THE REAL SURVIVO

ALSO FROM SIXTIES PRESS

EGPAC SERIES
Easy Guides for Patients and Carers

Kith and Kin – Experiences in Mental Health Caring
Beyond Stigma – Experiences of Mental Health
　　　　　　　　　Survivors

Forthcoming

Day Hospital Haven
Suicide and Near Suicide
How Trusts Work
Alcohol and Drug Dependency
Schizophrenia
Depression and Anxiety
Manic Depression
Personality Disorders
Medication and Mental Health
Talking Therapies
Art, Music and Drama Therapy
Care in the Community: Deliverance or Disaster?
Mental Health Today: Voices of Patients and Carers

THE REAL SURVIVORS ANTHOLOGY

POETRY FOR LIFE

edited by
Barry Tebb

SIXTIES PRESS 2006

© Individual authors
This Collection Copyright © 2006 Barry Tebb
ISBN: 0 9529994 6 3

Published by Sixties Press 2006
89 Connaught Road Sutton Surrey SM1 3PJ UK
&
27 Sefton Terrace Leeds LS11 7EL UK

www.sixtiespress.co.uk

This book owes its appearance entirely to the generosity of Awards for All

Cover photograph: Haworth Moor in autumn

Design and cover by Daisy Abey

*To Rowan Williams
poet and theologian
for his wisdom and humility*

Language is work
Hegel – *Phenomenology of Spirit*

CONTENTS

Daisy Abey   **21**
Voyages
Stranger
Haworth Moor
Lost Days
On Pennine Heights
 Comb
Lost Illusions
Paw Marks

Nela Abeygunawardana   **27**
Darkness
Beauty

Dileep Bagnall   **29**
Decades

Martin Bell   **30**
El Desdichado
A Benefit Night at the Opera
Usumcasane as Poet Maudit
A Prodigal Son for Volpone
The Enormous Comics
Verdi at Eighty
Words for Senilio to Work into a Patter-song

Joe Bidder   **36**
Neurologist
Blue in Green

Pat Bidmead   **40**
Against the Night

The Glass
Depression

Paul Birtill   **42**
Odd Behaviour
Sectioned

Thomas Blackburn   **43**
The Heart
Oedipus
The Maze
The Arrow and the Target
The Breaking Point
The Younger Son
The Lucky Marriage
All the Immortals
The Need for Dying
The Citizens: A Chorus from a Play
Hospital for Defectives
Trewarmett
Scenes from Childhood
Felo Da Se
An Aftermath
A Smell of Burning
Orpheus and Eurydice
A Small Keen Wind

Jane Bluett   **65**
2 am

Edwin Brock   **67**
When My Father Died
An Attempt at Exorcism

    In Memory of My Grandmother
    A Clutter of Mothers
    The Curtain Poem
    Five Ways to Kill a Man
    A Moment of Respect
    Unlucky Jim

John Butterworth   72
    To my Ideal Lady
    Dedicated to the Starving
    Invitation to Natural Beauty

Idris Caffrey   75
    White Room
    Getting Through

Margaret Theresa Carney   76
    Alice Living in the Looking Glass
    Reflections

Angela Carter   79
    My Cat in Her First Spring
    Life-affirming Poem
    The Horse of Love
    Poem for a Wedding Photograph
    Poem for Robinson Crusoe

Ken Champion   85
    Things

Debjani Chatterjee   86
    On a Midland Mainline Train
    Ruffled Feathers
    Hospital View

    Marilyn
    A Ghazal by Debjani Chatterjee
    Songs by Kazi Nazrul Islam
    Poems by Kazi Nazrul Islam

Kevin Crossley-Holland   **95**
    A Dream of a Meeting
    The Wall
    Confessional

Brian D'Arcy   **98**
    Trinity
    How Softly Sounds
    Returning Home
    Gone Like Dreams
    Remembering Anne
    Recumbent Stones at Arbor Lowe

Janet Fay   **103**
    Nightworkers

Mark Floyer   **104**
    English Teacher
    Blues
    Meccanosolitaire
    Edvoucayshun

Vanessa Freedman   **107**
    Broken
    Breakthrough

Anni G   **108**
    Words
    Reading

Geoffrey Godbert 109
    Therapy
    from About not Knowing

Jim Greenhalf 111
    Lone Wolf

Michael Haslam 114
    Spriggan Fair
    Vacations 1. iii
    Vacations 1. iv
    Vacations 1. v
    Schooling
    Green Withen Aura
    Two Poems from the Music
    The More Terrible Slips
    The Lucent School
    from A Century
    The Green Woodpecker

Anthony Hecht 130
    The Vow
    The Origin of Centaurs

Jonh Hirst 133
    Wilfred On War

Michael Holmes 134
    All Days Have Endings
    To Barbara (& the Beatles)

John Horder 136
    The Sick Image of My Father Fadesz

    Don't Postpone Amazing Yourself …
    The Measure of Their Fear
    My Muse Last Night
    A Sense of Being
    The Child Walks around its Own Grave
    In a Time When I was Nothing
    Love poem
    Why do They Never Cry?

Simon P. Jones   142
    Our Neil

Pat Jourdan   143
    Survivors

Jeanette Ju-pierre   144
    Ghost House

James Kirkup   145
    Homage to Ronald Firbank
    The Parting
    Fading Grass
    Waiting
    Amour de Tête
    Wreath Makers: Leeds Market
    Homage to Vaslav Nijinsky
    After Pentecost
    A Visit to Bronteland
    The Prodigal Son

Panayiota Konstantopoulou   153
    Socrates
    Remember
    Hors d'oeuvre

David Lambert   **155**
     Drinking from her Well
     Larkin's Curse
     British Tea for Boston Party
     Let's Write Barry a "White Sound" Open Reply

Neil Leadbeater   **158**
     The Long Goodbye
     My Last Afternoon with Mrs Pennwarden

Mike Loveday   **160**
     Rain
     Encounter in the Smoking Room

Daithidh Maccochaidh   **162**
     Sorrow
     Still

Anna Menmuir   **163**
     Love for Sale

Richard Middlebrook   **164**
     Final Intellectuals
     The Call of the Goddess
     I Spent this Afternoon
     Queen of Swords
     Queen of Cups

Maroushka Monro   **166**
     Seasonal Affective Disorder
     I Need to Know

Jim Moore   **169**
    At the 'Candles for the Holy Souls'
    The House and the Four Rogues
    The Lighting of Fires

Alan Morrison   **170**
    The Rosary Beads
    The Glove Compartment
    Mother Mouse
    Death's Breathtaking View
    Miss Discombobulated
    Intrusive Thoughts

Paul Murphy   **174**
    Images
    Snow
    Chamber Music

S. Nettle   **176**
    Doors
    Walking the Halls

Carolyn O'Connell   **178**
    Manifistations
    White
    Vortex

Wendy Oliver   **180**
    Out of Place
    Spell-breaking
    An End of Winter Night

Helen Overell   **185**
    Necklace

Mario Petrucci 186
    Mr. Haynes

Razz 187
    Dear God

Gerald Ryan 189
    Faith

John S. Savage 190
    The Angel has Grown Tired

Dolly Sen 191
    Queue

Jon Silkin 192
    Death of a Son
    To My Friends
    Furnished Lives
    The Return
    Respectabilities

James Simmons 199
    from Memorials of a Tour in Yorkshire
    The Dawning of the Day
    Flight of the Earls Now Leaving
    A Jig for Seamus
    My Friend the Famous Poet
    Geoffrey Hill
    Poor Tom
    The Rat Under The Roses
    The Road to Clonbarra

Stevie Smith   **207**
    Not Waving but Drowning
    The Suburban Classes

W.D. Snodgrass   **208**
    From Heart's Needle
    April Inventory
    The Marsh

Dave St. Clair   **218**
    How Many Reasons
    Closing the Shop
    Dear Barry
    The Return of the Future
    The Philosophies
    Big Brother Watching.
    The New Thing

Geoff Stevens   **224**
    Phalanger
    Pelota
    Point of Departure
    Hyena
    Pneumonicosis
    In the City at Night

Richard Stewart   **228**
    Hares at Fakenham Wood

Benito Stoakes   **229**
    My Father's Song

Elizabeth Tansley   **230**
    The Ward

Barry Tebb 232
    Reflecting on Wordsworth
    To the Sound of Violins
    Infamous Poet
    To the Memory of My Mother
    A Fine Madness
    To Daisy Abey
    Winterlight
    Paris
    This Used to be a Day Hospital
    The Road to Haworth Moor
    From Mooring Posts
    The Philosophers
    Death of a Poet

Bridget Temple-Jones 253
    Peace at last
    Something to Get Out of Bed for

Arcangelo Tinsley 254
    Hospital Blues

John Towers 255
    Best Day of Our Lives
    Night Terror

Daniel Tuohy 258
    Wonderful Life
    Redundant
    How Love Compels

Alex Warner 259
    Lonely

Julie Whitby **260**
    The Violet Room

Brenda Williams **261**
    Oxford from a Prison Cell
    Limen
    The Return
    from The Pain Clinic Part 1
    23 Fitzroy Road
    Untitled
    Royal Free Hampstead
    Primrose Hill
    For John Horder
    Dismantling Fordwych House
    from The Fields of Killingbeck
    Countertransference
    Nameless in Camden

Michael Williams **282**
    Old Woman

Lee Wilson **284**
    The Eternal Camera

June Worsell **285**
    Dandelions
    The Crimson Rose

John Younger **287**
    Case History
    American Dreams

Acknowledgements **289**

FOREWORD

All of us suffer from emotional distress when things go wrong. It could be loss of a close relative, a friend or even a family pet. Whether the loss was expected or not our memories live with us and it is hard to come to terms with our griefs. One in ten of us will spend some period of our lives, however short, on a psychiatric ward and almost all of us will ask our doctors for some form of medication to help us through life's all too many crises. In spite of these undeniable facts stigma still attaches to mental health, whatever the kind and whatever the cause.

When we are depressed, we lose our hopes, our self-confidence and feel that we will never get better. We feel tired and unwell with inner feeling of restlessness unable to concentrate, cope, sleep or relax. We can identify poetry with a companion who is willing to trust and communicate with us thoughtfully behind closed doors. Poetry helps deflect that haunting sadness and provides us a listener, carer and a sharer in itself to our own words and loneliness.

Reading and writing poetry has increasingly been found to alleviate mental pain, so much so that a qualification in poetry therapy has recently become available at a UK university, although it has been about in the USA for some years. As a poet, a patient and a carer it has been a labour of love to gather these poems together and present them to you, the reader.

Barry Tebb

DAISY ABEY

Voyages

As listless sun lays on
December burning fog
Planes fall from the sky
Rolling comets and shadows
Break the London silence
My mind trapped between
Palm trailed shores and
Scarlet tropic smoke.

Labyrinths of broad
Boulevards in grey Paris
Melt in windless rain
Unravelling eucalyptus
Melbourne rose in green.

I watched Ceylon seas screened
By haunting darkness, by ripples of
The sea, my childhood's horizon
The broken promises of absence
Cold, clammy, sand beneath my feet
As I turned away far from the night
Stars despondently shone.

Stranger

Between two centuries years falter,
Rainless July unfolded surging white
Heat waves sharpening the blades
Over the earth, on steps of days.

Stranger in a new green world
I wander alone along unseen tracks
Where nothing belongs to me yet I bear a burden
Of time passing, singing its own song.

In aeons beyond my being I imagine
The stars shining, the red rain overshadowing the sun's turn.

Whispering wind over moors haunting nights,
The tombs under the oaks so long forgotten.

Out of the darkness a spirit of the past emerges
Bearing a flickering blue lantern in its suppliant arms
Reflecting an azure glow dancing on mellow cobbles
Breathing the solemn air of long gone souls.

A child gathers pocketfuls of bilberries
Quizzically staring at desolate Pennine passes
She straddles a rocky cairn, showing her blood red palm
As ambling sea waves alter in their course.

Where all the time has gone, I cannot comprehend.
Along with the mother and father I once knew
Motes of dust glide in bronze sunbeams,
Unborn days echoing in my mind's core.

Haworth Moor

Magenta breeze over Haworth Moor
Whispers in the silence
The quiet of centuries darkens
The shadows of All Angels
Lichen roots on the tombstones
Gnarled elder, young wife, still-born child.

Penistone Hill overcast
Emptied the cobbled streets
The concrete pillar shook
Over the Brontes' bones
Their whispering ghosts
In the folded faded portrait
Ellis, Acton, Currer.

The white windmill turned
On the valley's side
As I walked down the Oakworth track
At twilight sunken in my own emptiness

Until I heard the trot of carriage horse,
The rumble of the passing hearse.

Lost Days

In Memory of Erna Fermie

The moments of an August silence ominous with breathless air
Screened in a corner hospital bed, a fan hums in the rising heat
Balancing the endless depths, you held down your final hours
Unable to accept eternity, a grown up child leaving home
When nothing is left but a blue haze divided in despair.

The road to *Woodend* still winds as I remember forty years
Midsummer mists of purple waving across lavender fields
Shadows of a mirage followed, darkening beneath my feet
Tremor of the descending sun, white crested trees
An empty house, an open gate, numb as winter nights.

Visitor to an unknown world, decades lost minutes to spare
Checking-in late, burdened by weight, the last train gone
Your hand trembles with terror, listening to an unheard song
A child's drawing on a wall *Granny come home*
But the leaf falls from its stem, wind blown in a storm.

This is the Edinburgh Festival you never made it to, an abrupt
Halt, that night of ceaseless rain, the dawn that never came
Declining the rhythm of breath, a gale force drowned in a sea
You held your hand, pulling towards the anchor of a
      floating feather
As tides recede to vacant years unveiled, a labyrinth of tears.

Filling this hollow time with memories of lost days
Where you walk on winter mornings along forsythia trails
Your daily route, past a vacant lot down St. Albans Way.
Now he wipes your brow; slowly you slipped away
With your restless eyes you mean something words cannot say.

The lonely evening followed by a night of strident wind
Whirling above your roof, damp paths hidden from daylight
Your silent journey to the chapel, a silence with vivid shapes
My heart crumbles from end to end covered in dank dust
That Friday, the sky loomed with cloud and infinite stars.

On Pennine Heights

Over the Pennine Heights
Centuries had passed in purple and white
Footmarks sunken in the gorge
Perfumed by moorland grass.

Wind moaned on cold winter nights
Tracks and rocks held their breath
Crumbled grains were frozen deep
The weight of a forgotten past.

Hills rose to a plateau then a sudden valley
Where timid sheep scattered over their moorland home
Here and there the grey stones of an abandoned farm
An aerial tapestry, a slowly moving stream.

Between the green of graves
A lonely fowl nested
As clouds hurried towards night
I heard the sound of silence.

Beyond the world I knew
Buried beneath all time
Lost among the livid shadows
My mind a broken leaf.

Comb

Worn out, unbreakable
Fifty years old
The comb that holds me
Until I am old.

Bronze-brown and nylon
You watched me turn grey
Travelled like a faithful dog
Love-in-a mist, never fades away.

For years I drowned in
Education for wisdom
You came, a gift from my father

Amid bags, drawers, holdalls
Teeth bright and smiling.

Now I sit touching you
Listening to your stories
Seeing through widening gaps
There are the fears in my mind
Our times combined.

Lost Illusions

O you most lovely image of my vision
O muse, come to me this perfect day
Stand guard by my flamingo gates
This last white winter grey.

O chimera of my lost illusions
Shadows metamorphosed by dreams unfold
Clear as the poignant stars by mist unrolled
Or gems enshrouded on a throne of gold.

What matters of the dreary days long gone
When zeniths of the summer sun unfold?
The zigzag crawling of a baby's gait
Brings glory to my lifetime not too late.

An August sun auger of the heather moors
And postcards from a poet in their lure
Striding the timeless tracks left by the gone
As still waters gleam serene and pure.

Our souls are thronged with airs
Of viols and vines, the reds of autumn splendour
Strum the ceaseless melodies azüre
And purple as the silence will endure.

Paw Marks

Eleven months since you had gone
The garden glazed in frost again
I look for your paw marks
Beneath the sand, on withered grass.

Magnolia is naked and listless
I hear you rustling fallen leaves
Your long howl at the hidden fox
I feel your presence day and night.

A shadow stands by a metal gate
Your territory is haunted
I walk alone no one at home
To greet me or to pass.

NELA ABEYGUNAWARDANA

Darkness

In my big black hole
Darkness is a beauty
Light,
A hidden heaven of dreams

You speak and I long to tell you my fears
I scream, I cry your name
But you can't hear me
Because I show you a make believe
I show you my hopes and dreams
As if they are real

When the longing is hard,
I hide from you
Hide but I fear the whole world can see
But then I wonder why
I cry when I hide from me

Slowly like my brother fading
I too stand and watch
I try and try to find the way,
This big black hole finds me for eternity.

I play that stupid melody in my head
Over and over again,
I laugh
Because there is no way
So I stand and wait
I'll watch you all go by,
Slowly slowly

Beauty

Loneliness is a pathway
My pathway of gradual sin
Empty as a nothing
Broken simile, broken heart
But even some angels decide to die
I guess you chose that long ago
You killed me from inside
But the angles are devils and you are dead
Words are the slurs running inside my head.
Beautiful
Red fragile succulent petals
Glistening in the morning light
Green finery, sways gently in the breeze
Beautiful
Little splat
Whoops silly me
One drop of blood
Little splat
Two drops of blood
Three four five six
Very bad me
I fall down
Still beautiful

DILEEP BAGNALL

Decades

The day he ate uncooked pasta
and almost burned down the flat.

The day he threatened people in town,
was medicated for that.

The day he nearly got run over
but laughed. In a dream, elsewhere.

The day he begged for cigarette money,
clearly not all there.

The day he prayed in church and heard
in his head the voice of God.

The day he was offered a job by the devil,
that opportunistic sod.

The day he took tablets and lay down to die.
The day he drew blood without thought for why.

The day he will show them, fools that they are.
Succeed like they just can't guess.

The day he will show them, by living a life
of worth and peace. Oh yes.

MARTIN BELL

El Desdichado

A gothicised version of Nerval

Look for me in the shadow, a bereft one, disconsolate,
Prince of Aquitaine and heir to a ruined Folly.
One star was mine, gone out now: my starred lute
Goes in dark circuit with the Sun of Melancholy.

O, to console me, in my graveyard midnight,
Bring back Posillipo and Italy's seas,
The flower that was my sad heart's favourite
And friends the rose and vine there, binding trellises.

Am I Eros, then, or Apollo? Lusignan or Byron?
My brow burns red still, which the Queen has kissed.
I have lingered in caverns where the sea-nymphs quire,

And twice, a conqueror, swum the straits of Acheron,
Mingling alternate strains on Orpheus' lyre,
Sighs of the anchorite, wailing of the possessed.

A Benefit Night at the Opera

The chatter thins, lights dip, and dusty crimson
Curtains start dragging away. Then, at one bound,
A rush of trumpets, ringing brass and vermillion -
The frescoed nymphs sprawl in a sea of sound.

We give our best attention as we must, for
This music is fatal and must be heard.
The glittering fountains vocalise our lust,
The whole brilliant scene sways on to murder.

The idyll interrupted by a cough,
Coloratura soars into a fever.
After the vows, the sibyl shuffles off,
The conspirators' chorus mutter, melt away, leave us

A traitor and his stabbed tyrant, downstage in tears.
Masked revellers are grouping for a wedding.
In stern beat start to life six scarlet halberdiers,
Move with the music, march to a beheading.

Lo! Wild applause proclaims a happy ending.
Vendetta is achieved with clinking swords.
Sheer from the battlements the Diva is descending,
Rash in black velvet and resplendent chords.

Usumcasane as Poet Maudit

> Is it not brave to be a king, Techelles,
> Usumcasane, and Theridamas?
> Is it not passing brave to be a king
> And ride in triumph through Persepolis?

Noses in books, odd children in good schools
Get praise by being clever. And they sing
Revenge on the fortunate, the easy-going fools;
And think it passing brave to be a king.

King then, but of words only. There's the rub.
Action is suspect and its end uncertain:
Stuck in a Job, or browned off in a pub,
Or fêted and then stabbed, behind a Curtain...

Impatiently they strain their eyes
To see small faults through powerful lenses:
Angrily snatch at paradise,
Exacerbating their five senses.

Famous young Rimbaud managed rather better -
Crammed all he could beneath his greedy hide,
Went to Abyssinia, wouldn't write a letter:
Was made into a saint before he died.

A Prodigal Son for Volpone

Conspicuous consumption? Why, Volpone
Would splash it around as if he could afford it,

Wore himself out for his craft, a genuine phoney,
Who only wanted, gloatingly, to hoard it.

His son had sprung like a mushroom, pale in an alley.
Reluctant, they had to unload the stuff on him.
To cook the accounts, got Mosca back from the galleys -
These lawyers worried that the heir looked dim.

What was he, now, to do with all this gold?
His father had withered in prison because of it.
Root of all evil, he'd always been told
By scholars who'd brought him up. Get shot of the lot of it.

Gloomy vaults, cram-full roof-high with piles
Of metal and stone and paper shoved into sacks:
A great city's sewer, bustling golden miles
Swollen for carnival. Must give it back,

Somehow get rid of it, be a big spender.
The tradesmen knew of a new purse spilling around.
Not a junk-shop in Venice that wasn't stripped of its splendour,
Not a period-piece, not an objet d'art to be found.

How richly the monde assembled at his parties,
How thickly clustered in slow gilded whirls!
Sensitive businessmen and butch aesthetic hearties,
Senile young statesmen, faint expensive girls.

'Spend it faster?' He'd pay on the nail for their answers.
A patron's deep-waving harvest was quick to be seen.
A sculptor in barbed-wire, a corps of Bulgarian dancers,
Three liberal reviews and a poetry magazine.

Mosca's smirk broadened. The Foundation showed a profit.
How white and stammering now our Volponetto!
'G-give it to the city. S-see the poor get some of it.'
He vanished aboard a waiting vaporetto.

For one odd halfpenny, Mosca broke on the rack.
The Senate's liver was hardened with golden wine.
Some money drained to the poor. The young man never came back.
Last heard of, was herding swine, or turned to swine.

The Enormous Comics
A Teacher to his Old School

Barnacled, in tattered pomp, go down
Still firing, battered admirals, still go down
With jutting jaw and rutting tooth and tongue,
Commanding order down cold corridors.

Superbly, O dyspeptic Hamlets,
Pause in the doorway, startle the Fourth Form
With rustlings of impatient inky cloaks -
Time and time again you go into your act.

Benevolent and shaven, county cricketers,
Heroes on fag-cards, lolling out of the frame,
Or smug and bun-faced, Happy Families,
Or swollen in shrill rage (Off With His Head!),

You lean huge areas into close-up
With cruel pampered lips like Edward G.
Robinson, or Tracy's anguished eyes,
And still remain the seediest of grandees.

Processioned hierarchically, larger than life,
Gigantic Guy Fawkes masks, great heads on stilts -
Your business was traditional, strictly articulated
Into timetables, only a few steps

From nightmare. Wild clowns will terrify
Wagging a wooden phallus at the crowd,
Raising a roar of response, of love and loathing -
Fat scapegoats stuck with broad rosettes of learning.

I listened and made myself little, still as a mouse
Watching the growling pussies at their antics -
Now I see, in the back row of any classroom,
Sharp impatient eyes, weighing me up for the drop.

Large masks creak. Sir will tear a passion to tatters.
One must pray for unobstructed moments,
For chances to be useful,
Like theirs, old wretches, like theirs.

Verdi at Eighty

1.

My brides are ravished away, are ravished away,
Two Leonoras, Gilda, Violetta,
One swaggering tenor has taken them,
One death seduced them to fever.
I have contrived a basso politics
To hunt him down, conspired
Through trio and quartet, strong situations,
Needled him on to my avenging sword.

2.

How shall a wicked, fat, old man be saved?
Connive with the women, incessant giggles and whispers.
He must be re-baptised in muddy water
And wash the district's dirty linen with him.
The wine will chirrup, an insect in old veins.
Ready then assume the sacrificial horns,
Grovel in terror before the Fairy Queen,
So that, our hope, lost lovers may re-join:
Nanetta find a tenor in the woods.
The festival will glow in basso nimbus of laughter.

Words for Senilio to Work into a Patter-song
My body is a broad and blossoming meadow.
    Vivian de Sola Pinto

1.

My body is a relief map in eruption
Wrinkles wrinkles wrinkles riddle the landscape
Pimples keep on erecting and detumescing all the time
My face swells and subsides and always finishes older
I have one or two grey hairs among the hairs around my testicles
I give my eyeballs everyday marks for yellowness and bloodshotness
I blow my nose hard each morning to find out how deaf I am
My handkerchiefs are filled with snot
When I make love I do it fiercely several nights in a row

As if it were the last time each time
Then go on the booze for a fortnight
Insulting my dear wife with silences

2.

When I wake at four in the morning
There are always two landscapes inside
One is the mess one has made of one's human life
(I can say it only in dreams
I am always trapped in the leaking submarine, the executioner taps
    on the door
I am always back at school or in the army
Having lost my rifle not read Beowulf)
Two is the gurgling and splashing and undermining in the bowels
The snuffle in the bronchi and the sinuses
Orchestrating with bloody birds and aeroplanes outside
Cancer has captured this town and that town one says

3.

One gets up makes tea
Discusses the possible public image with the shaving-mirror
Trims the beard sharp

One walks into the sunlight rehearsing wisecracks

One's wife will, mercifully, give one breakfast
Consents to gossip.

JOE BIDDER

Neurologist

Like a scientist
you examine my body,
probe for weakness,
measure incapacity,
refer to your notes.

Like a solicitor
you say nothing
until pushed hard;
prefer to measure
response and reaction,
judge the brain's efficiency
by set-piece standards.

Like a specimen,
pickled in a jar,
my flesh awaits
the next test;
"follow that finger
press this hand
walk that line"

I know; know
better than you,
that bits don't function
the way they used to,
the way they should.
I'm scared that one day
the bits won't work at all;
that legs, arms, eyes
larynx and genitals,
will finally cease to function.
And on that day you will write
in your precious file
science has been vindicated,
that you were right.

Like a penitent
I used to wait on your ward
hoping against hope for hope
but you said nothing.
I begged for information,
the test results from
the National Hospital,
but those you disallowed.
Like a medieval priest
you clutch knowledge
close to skin,
as if to withhold
the meaning of life,
but all along
you know so little.
The scans and
magnetic resonances
show that neurons are dead,
but you don't know why.

Like a zombie
I reeled before
the blank wall
of the unsaid,
often wishing
I had instead
a broken leg
or blocked arteries:
something tangible
we could comprehend -
that doctors could cure.

Like an automaton
you can only repeat
your predictable tests,
silently prod and probe,
make fresh notes, then whisper
to the ubiquitous student,
who, one day - no doubt,
will probe in silence -
just like you.

Like Lazarus I rise
from the bed of despair
determined to fight.
I rely on homeopath
and healer to inspire
the rhythm of survival.

Like a neurologist
you observe my spirit.
Although you offer
no hope or prognosis
you encourage me to write.
Unlike you
I put my thoughts
on paper
for all to read.

Blue in Green

Slanted rain against evening sun
Depressing, yet this is not despair.
Sun bounces off slick paths. Plangent
- like Miles Davis' *Sketches of Spain*

and my 1961 pilgrimage
to the Cimitière Père Lachaise wall
terminated In Clichy by a detour
to buy *Kind of Blue*, which dominates

the shelf In its original cover, grooves
pitted by ten million revolutions;
Miles' trumpet on Blue in Green
and John Coltrane's tenor on *So What*,

Speaking of Coltrane, the rain has stopped
and the sun's reflection now glares; tough,
hard-edged, sheets of sound, stretched
harmonics and a tender cry originating

somewhere between Savannah and Sahara.
I lay on my bed for hours, replaying
Giant Steps for the kick in the groin,
dependent on that frisson of elation.

Rain and sun, sun and rain - again.
The velvet grass sings, shimmers; stems
sparkle, spiral the violet-blue sky.
Miles and Trane are dead» but not in despair.

PAT BIDMEAD

Against the Night

I hang a curtain against the night,
A screen before the years of no escape,
And across the open window of my soul
I drape a lace netting of tears
So I can filter the light through my experience,
But in the garden outside
The crazy paving stones of love
Lie sliced through,
And the shattered concrete groans
As a gravelled ache rattles
Against the half awake senses,
And the cold rake of reality drags gritted pain
Through wire mesh fences of extra sensitivity.
You have gone and nothing can remain
But a painful memory caught in the curtain,
That even now is uncertain
Of hanging against the night
That closes in on me.
And on the other side of the tears
Will the uncried pain find no relief
In the dried remains of my grief,
Dusting the bare brick years
Where beneath the brittle conversation
A cold wind rakes
The abandoned building site,
And grates the hinges of iron night against
The unseen trees
Wearing their cement leaves,
When I pass will they always
Shake their unforgiving dust
Into my drinking glass of living?

The Glass

Where the mountain side of distress
Wears the thin trees
Like a hanging beard of despair,
How easy to bless the wine

And raise the glass
To ease the ache
To break the pain,
Till all too soon
There is a glass to make
Each tension filled day
Praise non living,
But relief that borrows
From the glass
Is repaid by tomorrow's reality
When the glass no longer eases the ache
For the ache now needs
The glass to break
Against its own mountain of pain.

Depression

I see the future in double vision
When depression hangs limp on my brow,
Trouble and pain in collision
Can only follow me now
Into a tomorrow that's hollow
And bare.
I hear a double echo
When depression haunts my present,
And how it rebounds from walls of despair
To know the agony
Of the spirit it can only drain
With its repetition inside my brain.
I live a double ache
When depression sweeps low
My morale and enters my very soul
Causing a double break
In all that I know.

PAUL BIRTILL

Odd Behaviour

Just recently I've taken to putting
up two fingers at funeral corteges,
and have been beaten up several times.
My Psychiatrist tells me it's just a
phase I'm going through - a kind of
mid-life crisis, not unusual for a
man of my age and background. I asked
him was it common, and he said in some
pprts of India it occurs quite a lot
and referred me to the School of Tropical
Medicine.

Sectioned

They stand around me in
a big circle - arms folded
faces expressionless. I try
to explain that I'm not mad
and it's all a big mistake
I plead my case strongly -
passionately as if my life
depended on it; and just
when I think I've won them
over - convinced them I'm sane
this big black guy jabs me.

THOMAS BLACKBURN

The Heart

At the woman in the valley
I shook an angry fist,
For she damned the summer starlight
And when my lovers kissed
Brought bell and book and candle
And drove them out of town;
But the stars sang, it is you condemn them,
Oh, pull your own heart down.

She stood in her red garment
Like a thorn in the side of day,
Eros on his golden beaches
Grew sickly and bled away.
I knelt by his spent body
And cherished his vine-leaved crown;
But the god said, it is you condemn me,
Oh, pull your heart down.

She came like a frost and the dancers
Grew stiff as she raised her arm.
The drums, the flutes and the trumpets
Hushed in a dead-sea calm.
Why do you shatter this music,
And let my sweet-hearts drown?
It is you, said the dancers, you are the Gorgon,
Oh, pull your own heart down.

Alone in the sweating metal
Of her parental tower,
Danae knelt and beyond her
Circled the nuptial power.
This long cold night of the brasses
No morning star will crown;
It is you, you, you, she cried, you are my prison;
Oh, pull your own heart down.

Oedipus

His shadow monstrous on the palace wall.
That swollen boy, fresh from his mother's arms,
The odour of her body on his palms,
Moves to the eyeless horror of the hall.

And with what certainty the Revelation
Gropes for the sage's lips; words whine and bark
Out of that crumpled linen in the dark
To name the extremity of violation.

How should he not but tremble as the world
Contracts about him to his mother's room
Red-curtains, stifling; in the fire-lit gloom
His swollen manhood on her bed is curled.

Then up and blind him, hands, pull blackness down
And let this woman on the strangling cord,
Hang in the rich embroidery other gown;
Then up and blind him, pull the blackness down.

But as he stumbles to the desert sands,
Bleeding and helpless as the newly born
His daughters leading him with childish hands
1 see beyond all words his future shape,
Its feet upon the carcass of the ape
And round its mighty head, prophetic birds.

The Maze

1.

To-night that thirsting girl glides through the town,
With nervous footsteps from the royal door,
Crushed ivy, liquid music in her mouth,
To mate a beast upon the sea's cold shore.

White on the salted margin she lies down,
'Darkness, now take me, now, Darkness'; she sighs.
Slowly it breeds upon her, throbs, grows full,
The spirit carnal in a panting bull,

Straddles her body with its heavy thighs.

The morning breaks; upon the trampled sand,
Blood crusted to her side, foam in her hair.
She drops blue pebbles from an idle hand,
Sunlight reflected in her calm blank stare.

And then they find her; she can't speak at all,
Giggles and points her tongue, she plays bo-peep,
Crawls crab-like on the earth, begins to weep,
Blasted and burnt out like a terminal.

Fused, the mind broken; how could she that stress
Of loaded voltage, beating hammer blows,
Redeem with her untutored nakedness.
It craved the pattern of a psychic rose,
Steel petalled, to transform its savage need
To hallowed energy; well some must bleed.
I like to think they took her home to rest,
Wiped her quite clean and fed her, till that day,
Matted with ochre fur, the man-beast lay
And whimpered naked on her childish breast.

2.

Cell by small cell from that increasing core,
Unceasing night or day, this people's guilt
Raised stone on stone, until their fear had built
A labyrinth about the Minotaur.

But still its passion to the outer wall
Stretched nervous tendrils, though it wandered blind
And mindless in the caverns of the mind;
Rest but a moment and they heard it call.

Most piercing when the last autumnal days
Rose calm and golden, then it shook the ground,
Craving for sacrifice; blindfold and bound,
They sent their sons and daughters to the maze.

The children screamed, then muttered undertones;
Above the worshippers, that royal pair

Saw blood rise steaming in the frosty air,
Cold as the icy marble of their thrones.

3.

Gently across a palm the nervous thread
Unreels its knowledge, as his other hand,
Muscled and delicate, just strokes the wall,
Learning the secrets of this buried land,
The speech in stones of his ancestral dead,
Their fears in dust the centuries let fall.

Deeply he penetrates; the air grows stale,
Heavy and odorous with gathering storm.
It is the beast which makes the darkness warm
And in its reeking breath his sinews fail,
His manhood melts, in terror now he flies
Leaping the last defences of the heart,
To sink in tears upon the arena's floor;
Towering above its prey, the Minotaur
Looks down on Theseus with pale, hungry eyes.

4.

In the stone ring to-night. I see this pair
In breathless nuptials, as if they made,
Yoked to the opposite each could not bear,
A single creature, till all colours fade
Out of the Labyrinth and their bodies drown.
It is this mutual dying calls you down,
Light, dear and terrible whose childish hands
Once troubled our first waters, now like birds
Fluttering and nestling on the monster's spine.
Your operation turns its blood to wine
And draws it foaming through each broken wrist
Of Theseus hanging on the carnal tree
Which pours into its fruit. He drops and sways,
Alone, the newborn light by dark increased,
Then steps alive and naked from the Beast,
Its fell, his radiancy, out of the Maze.

The Arrow and the Target

The arrows that we loose abroad
Shall never find their mark
Until they whistle back to us
Out of the random dark.
Till the arrow and the target,
The archer and the bow
Are married in a single act,
Fond lovers only know
The light of a wax taper
High on a swinging tree,
Or a ring on a green finger
Under the choking sea.

The arrows of the archer
Are pointed with his need
But when the target is transfixed
His body too must bleed,
Because there is a single act
In which they still both share,
Though disunited by a tense
Which makes them here and there.
To bring that action to itself
Out of each fractured part,
The arrows must go singing from
The bowstring of the heart.

The arrow for the target,
The archer for the bow
And each heart for the nuptials
True lovers only know,
Who wear upon one finger
The gold ring of the sea
And pluck down their wax taper
Out of the swinging tree.

The Breaking Point
for James Smyth

They say an Indian princeling asked a hermit
Of what men are the shadows and was told

To fetch him from a spring a little water,
But when he brought the cup back had grown old.
Down there, it seems, he met a herdsman's daughter
And dreaming in her arms forgot his quest,
Until catastrophe lurched through his garden
And wrenched the child and woman from his breast.
Then once again he stood before his master,
Who took the cup and murmured, "All this while
To fetch me from a spring a little water."

It's simple isn't it, you wake and smile.
That's if your dream breaks; but just now its creatures
Seem very real to me, as every day
Come rattling from my heart those angry shadows
That are themselves and do not melt away.
And though I know what rounds into completeness
This dream-the rage and hunger-can disguise
The vision of the hermit in the silence,
Still they continue to put out his eyes.

At least I think it comes, the stricken vision
Which penetrates the foliage of a dream,
From fire and sword, the voltage of disaster
Which shocks us through the landscape as we scream.
For how should we wake up and see our master
Unless the bones and leaves that hid his face
Are cancelled out by such deliberate dying?
We must diminish for his living space.
And yet although I'm sure the dream's a fiction
Which doubtless it is better to see through,
It rules the clocks and cobble-stones we walk on,
And when we've found its platitudes untrue
What breathes them out and murmurs in their language
May be reality but is elsewhere.
I wonder what the princeling did the morning
After his house and home had turned to air?

He may have understood the master's vision,
And daylight streaming through his emptiness,
Have walked abroad among the hooded sleepers
And clarified their landscape of distress.
But often when the dream has broken open

And let our circumstance drop out of time,
We turn and seek again that breathless moment,
Here where the maps are and where real clocks chime.

Oh, drunkards, seeking in the dirt eternal
Unfathomed energies no fact can bear,
Who scrabble headlong through the roots of being
For that which is itself and is elsewhere,
When shall you stand before your quiet master,
Who takes the cup and murmurs, "All this while
To fetch me from a spring a little water,"
And look upon your ravaged dream and smile?

The Younger Son
for G. Wilson Knight

The crowns return to dust, the sweetmeats vanish,
When the third son with his deliberate eye
Looks coldly through the banquet and the bauble
And proves the witch's palace is a lie.
But always, as in solitude and silence
He takes his stick and buckles on his load,
He sees the two grey dolmens of his brothers
Beside the deprivation of the road.

They did not understand the glare and music
To which they spurred their horses through the night
Were not the goal itself, but only beacons
To keep their passion of the quest alight,
And when some gaudy woman of the palace
Threw down her handkerchief and made sweet moan,
Each clattered up the stairs into her bedroom
And on the stroke of midnight turned to stone.
The journey was itself their occupation
And not some minion of a torchlit hall;
Of course the heart must beat, the pulses quicken
Or there's no road or journeying at all,
But still a certain irony is needed.
I mean that when the princess is awake,
The younger son who sought her in the forest
And plucked her jewel from the haunted lake
Is quick to guess, there, at the crux of passion,

The journey was not merely for a bride,
But some new clarity that rinsed his nature
When he cut through the brambles to her side.

But only his obedience to the language
Of birds and suppliant fishes by the way
Can yield the hero that momentous secret
Which topples giants headlong to the clay.
The elder sons exchange such night time murmurs
For the new guide-book of some master hand,
Then take the hopeless turning at the cross-roads
And walk their lives out in a waste of sand.

Now, by the monolith before the castle,
The third son hears the slug-horn fade and die,
Then gasps at the great bastion of those shoulders
A league above him in the punished sky.
No wonder as earth shook and giant fingers
Groped slowly inward through the forest trees,
His brothers, lost within their own phantasma,
Went headlong into blindness on their knees.
For saplings bend, rocks split, the grass is ravished,
When to the urgent summons of that horn
Some passion of the heart rears out of silence
To drench our landscape with its furious dawn.
Then only those whom birds and fish have tutored
Can hold their upright posture by the stone,
Because they know the energies that nourish
The passion of the monster are their own.
This is the younger son's most precious secret;
And may we also hear the trapped bird cry
And be rewarded by a naked vision
When our appalling manias shake the sky.

The Lucky Marriage

I often wonder as the fairy story
Tells how the little goose-girl found her prince,
Or of the widowed queen who stopped her carriage
And threw a rose down to the gangling dunce,
What is the meaning of this lucky marriage
Which lasts forever, it is often said,

Because I know too well such consummation
Is not a question of a double bed,
Or of the wedding bells and royal procession
With twenty major-domos at its head.

At least its bride and groom must be rejected;
The fairy godmother will only call
On Cinders scrubbing tiles beside the chimney
While her proud sisters foot it at the ball;
From all but the last son without a birthright
The beggarwoman hoards her magic seed.
Well, if they'd had the good luck of their siblings
And found occasion kinder to their need,
They would have spent their breath on natural pleasures
And had no time for murmurs in the night:
They heard because they were condemned to silence,
And learnt to see because they had no light.

I mean the elder son and cherished sister
Know but the surface of each common day;
It takes the cunning eye of the rejected
To dip beneath that skin of shadow-play
And come into the meaning of a landscape.
I think that every bird and casual stone
Are syllables thrust down from some broad language
That we must ravel out and make our own.
Yet who is ever turned towards that journey
Till deprivations riddle through the heart?
And so I praise the goose-girl and the scullion
Beside a midden or a refuse cart.

And yet all images for this completion
Somehow by-pass its real ghostliness
Which can't be measured by a sweating finger,
Or any salt and carnal nakedness.
Although two heads upon a single pillow
May be the metaphor that serves it best,
No lying down within a single moment
Will give the outward going any rest;
It's only when we reach beyond our pronouns
And come into ourselves that we are blest.
Is this the meaning of the lucky marriage

Which lasts forever, it is often said,
Between the goose-girl and the kitchen servant,
Who have no wedding ring or mutual bed?

All the Immortals

Walking, catlike, between the imperatives,
Battering against iron bars and wood and stone,
Staring red-eyed through all correlatives
Into the heart of 'Being' and their own,
I think of those who found it hard to be human -
Beethoven raging, splintered within his head
The intolerable details of correct behaviour,
While to enter his brain and be interpreted
Yearned a celestial but disordered order
Baudelaire coupling on a dirty bed
With the antithesis of his Beata,
'Pour contempler mon coeur... et sans dégout,
Seigneur, donnez-moi la force et le courage,'
That Dutchman posting off his severed ear,
Swift stalking through his intolerable dotage,
The mob's delight, spectacle and spectre:
'All the Immortals,' Yeats said, and all the Immortals,
Their salt-cut hands, their broken eyes that stare
Through the minute particulars of knowledge
Into the daemon of phenomena,
Who else these Lenten days should one remember?

The Need for Dying
And the wolf said, 'You must kill me.' (Fairy story)

They could not have outstripped the witch's daughter,
Got up unpoisoned from the ogre's feast,
Or fished the queen's lost ring out of the water,
Without this suppliant and gentle beast,
Who, since they gave it bread and pulled the thorn out,
Lent all its secret wisdom to their quest,
Forgave them each misdeed until one morning
Beyond their foul enchantment they were blest.

But then it turns towards the ransomed lady
And sea-changed princeling, whom no spells could part,

And murmurs earnestly, 'And now the promise,
Take your bright sword and plunge it in my heart.'
Of course they shrink away and offer riches,
Broad water-meadows and a golden stall,
But at the last yield to the beast's imploring
And deal the fatal stroke that severs all.

Out of its blood then and the rags and tatters
Of fur and membrane on the stubble corn,
All glistening on his new most lucky morning,
A second time the king's charmed son is born.
He needed such a death stroke to redeem him
From reptile, animal or bird of prey;
And yet without his creature and its knowledge
How could the spell-bound children find their way
Through all those convolutions of a forest?
His night it was that guided them each day.

I mean that always on our star-crossed journey
That which we are is helpless to decide
Between a sheep track and a posted highway,
Until we drop the reins and cease to guide
Our pacing animals who smell direction
Blown softly through the gap where our will died.
No whip or spur of furious intention
But checks their speed, unravelling the dark,
And if the master bellows out his orders,
Before the abyss, then, no hound will bark.
I think he is the night, this charmed companion,
And that in dreams and blood he lends us speech
And seeing, with no eyes, that catch a meaning
Our organs of the day could never reach,
If, humble as the lovers of the story,
We bend down low to his insistent breath
And turn a deaf ear to the witch's calling.
But why must we reward him by his death,

The faithful guide who led us through confusion?
Well, all the rituals say that he must die,
This creature of the night, and his blind wisdom
Be changed within the twinkling of an eye.
I do not think his fish, white wolf or stallion

Have any knowledge of their future lord;
They only know that when their task is finished
They seek the desolation of the sword.
Perhaps, one day, we'll leave the witch's kingdom
And thrust our childhood foliage apart;
Oh, may we then be altar, priest and victim,
A sharp, bright clarity, and pierce the heart.

The Citizens: A Chorus from a Play

After the marsh was drained and its vast monsters
Had gasped their lives out in the well-rinsed air,
Our city corporation cleaned the fosse up
And charged us sixpence to see Grendell's lair.
We thought that with the Great Panjandrum banished
An era of sweet dreams was sure to start;
But gracious no, only his cave has vanished;
Don't look now, but he's walking in your heart.

After Sir Hercules had combed the mountains
And killed the Nemean lion, our woods were bare.
On feast days now we can go out to picnic
And if it rains take shelter in its lair;
The pebbles and the moss are quite enchanting.
I think I hear the ancient roaring start.
What's that you say? I said the ancient roaring,
Excuse me but it's coming from your heart.

Upon our museum shelves we keep the omens
That after school before they go to bed
Children may see some curious time-worn bauble
A pickled toad, a stone, a Gorgon's head.
Why do they cry in sleep, the silly children,
Of birds that speak, of snakes that hiss and dart
Upon a woman's scalp? Put them to silence.
You cannot stop the language of the heart.

In days gone by the warriors would sit feasting,
Then freeze to silence at the slow footfall
Of Grendell's furious dam who rocked the postern,
Then strode through snapping beams into the hall.
That monster comes no more by field or river,

But still our dwelling-place is torn apart
By human hands - like mine - our children ravaged;
Oh, hide me from the fury of the heart.

Hospital for Defectives

y your unnumbered charities
A miracle disclose,
Lord of the Images, whose love,
The eyelid and the rose
Takes for a language, and today
Tell to me what is said
By these men in a turnip field
And their unleavened bread.

For all things seem to figure out
The stirrings of your heart,
And two men pick the turnips up
And two men pull the cart;
And yet between the four of them
No word is ever said
Because the yeast was not put in
Which makes the human bread.
But three men stare on vacancy
And one man strokes his knees;
What is the meaning to be found
In such dark vowels as these?

Lord of the Images, whose love,
The eyelid and the rose
Takes for a metaphor, today
Beneath the warder's blows,
The unleavened man did not cry out
Or turn his face away;
Through such men in a turnip field
What is it that you say?

Trewarmett
for Julia Blackburn

Darkness, feathers are shed;
These birds are gathered back

By the enormous hand
That cast them at dawn seaward
In crumbs of living bread
To their forefathering rock.

Piercing the lens of a wave,
From the beat of it and the swell,
The feathered life they have
Is indivisible,
As from the undertow
And skin of a nervous sea
Fish and themselves also
They reap perpetually.
Being clothed, and without a seam,
In the pouring waters they thread,
How can they miss their aim,
By the loose surge targeted
Forever towards their home?

Darkness, feathers are shed;
From this bird-whitened stone,
I watch a cormorant pluck
Life from a nervous sea,
With a moon behind my back,
Conscious of God knows what
Anxious irrelevance
As these birds swim in the eye
Of the green circumstance
From which I am undone
By my duplicity.

Watching a bird, and a man
Watching a bird in the surf,
Watched by a man, and that faint
Rim of horizon far off
Where darkness breeds from a glint
Of metal, I wait for the tide
To work its equation out.
Through hunger, compulsive dread,
Are ghosts forever unlaid
By a moon's impetus
That takes the sea by the throat,

I assert, as it gathers up all
Of night to one moment of stress
That is perpetual,
My own self-consciousness.
The waters boom and rave;
Being human, what else can I have
Than such good and growing pain,
Between the living and dead,
On this sea-shaken stone?

Scenes from Childhood

1.

The stain was obvious, his father said,
Though with great caution he might somehow hide
Cain's mark upon his forehead, and the beast
Ready to leap and swamp him like a tide.
The thing was to assume a decent pose,
To shake hands firmly, keep the hair brushed down,
Even a bishop might then condescend
Thinking the animal but harmless clown.
With dog-like gratitude he did his best,
Kept all his buttons fastened, pared his nails,
Was always ready to sit on the lawn
And listen to old ladies telling tales.
But every night behind a close locked door,
He took a razor blade then slashed his thigh,
The hot blood hissed and steamed into a pail;
He fell asleep, but dreaming wished to die.

2.

As mother's darling nothing was withheld,
Long bedtime stories, rambles in the park,
Each wish became a shining toy, her hand
Was always there to soothe him in the dark.
One thing was negative; the cellar door
Must not be opened. How could he deny
That small obedience in a yielding world,
And bring a tear to the all loving eye.
He walked with caution always above ground,

But nights are wild though days seem calm and dry:
In dreams he went by silent stairs and came
To that one door, and wakened with a cry.
Dreams are not alien; he grew afraid
Of something close and waiting, one can't tell
The least stray image might benumb the mind
Till drunken footsteps reach the gates of Hell.
All smiling flower-set pathways can betray
Weak erring children to that darkened room,
He burned both shoes and trousers and lay still
Sobbing and helpless on the nursery floor.
But heard quite clearly, with a fever's sense,
The key turn quietly in the cellar door,
Then heavy footsteps mount from stair to stair;
The sweat ran down his face and through his hair.

3.

'Rains beat the window, but this room is warm
Its curtains blot the night out, and the night
Is where they walk who left the sheltering light,
And pace about our house, blind in the storm.'
They said this and then spoke of trivial things,
But he could see their hands crooked like a claw
The terror in her eyes that tried to smile,
But always watched the windows and the door.
The fire burned out and they both ceased to talk,
Then in the silent room they seemed to rise,
And stare upon him with calm, maniac eyes.

4.

His power was absolute in her domain
To be half Anthony, a wasteless God,
Whose every childish antic could obtain
The great obeisance, the maternal smile.
Price of that power none noticed in her room,
One could forget if outside in the sky
Storm piled on angry storm cloud, cold and dark;
Within her arms how warm it was and dry.
But growth in time continues, and he came
Close to that world of man we can't deny

And weeping was drawn slowly to a stage
Of different vision to his mother's eye.
Here the one need seemed what she could not bear
The gallery screamed out and roared him down;
He threw away his Hamlet hat and played
A novel character, half beast, half clown.

5.

It seemed there had been something back in time;
 Lost now, but loving faces seemed to show
A fear of repetition and a crime
His memory had covered up like snow.
They watched him tenderly, made simple rules,
'Avoid excitement, never walk by night',
And he grew to them closely, terrified
Of something lurking in him out of sight.
On whose monstrosity they drew a veil,
Prayed, wept and fasted, cut each sprouting hair,
Until he grew so gentle and so pale
They felt the certainty of answered prayer.
But as they sat one evening by the fire,
Proud of the son safe in their loving bands,
The storm broke in him; laughing, blind,
He came down to them with enormous hands.

6.

By dusty corridors he goes to court
Disaster, with the footsteps of a child.
We plead and reason, but we cannot change
His terrible intention to the dark.
That has the final logic of disease
Taking his being slowly in its sway,
We can but watch him move to the eclipse,
Then from his destination turn away.
For he has now descended the last stair,
His fingers open the forbidden door,
We hear him scream out once and then no more.

Felo Da Se

'Thirty,' the doctor said, 'three grains, each one,
That's quite a lot of sodium-amytol!
Five, ten more minutes, and the job was done,
Just why do you think she wished to end it all?
Ah, well, that's not my business. You've her things?
Damn lucky that I had the stomach pump -
Take them up to her if the Sister rings.'
I thanked him and agreed the night was damp,
Then flicked through Punch and waited the event;
It was, you see, no time for sentiment.

Her things, though, had been much in evidence
Back in the flatlet when I searched through drawers
To find a nightgown (blue is for romance)
And her remembered hairbrush through such tears
As in these situations must be shed -
(It is the cause, my soul, it is the cause)
I found her slippers underneath the bed
Where we had . . . where she drained her bitter cup
In solitude the night before this night;
What mattered was to pack a suitcase up,
Put out the light, 'and then put out the light'.
'So,' the nurse said, 'you've come. She may go out.'
I noticed that my shoe-lace was untied,
But though some words climbed up into my throat
Found none appropriate to suicide;
I took her arm, though, like a helpful friend
And led her downstairs to the waiting car,
Thinking, our game we do not understand
Nor who is playing it or what we are,
Her landlord came in time and that was luck.
I changed the gear. Who drives behind my back?

Her friend was waiting for us at the flat
With tea and so on. This I had arranged.
Knowing too well such passion spun the plot,
Death was its end unless the scene was changed,
What could I do but tear apart the script
Which made quite clear the end of our impasse?
As, kneading with her hands, she sat white lipped,

(There are some shadows which take long to pass)
Her friend poured tea, and slowly, drop by drop,
In solitude we drained our acid cup.

We had exhausted words as well as touch,
Therefore at half past ten I said goodbye,
Breaking the silence with a lifted latch,
To join, once more, my own identity.
That night the chilly street was not as dark
With its faint lamp as my intelligence,
And since more suited is a question mark
Than a full-stop, to human ignorance,
The blue stone I recall on her left hand;
Just what it means I do not understand.

An Aftermath

They hadn't noticed her coming, too busy with loud
Out-goings, that savage night, his wife and he;
Two's company, you know, but three's a crowd,
And the upthrust and draught of fantasy
Leave little room a child can hope to fill.
Evil each saw and nothing else could see,
The two of them were dead if looks could kill;
And then they turned and saw her balanced there
Upon the spinning rim of their nightmare.

I'd like to think it shook them to a pause,
Their daughter, her shut face, but that's not true;
Nothing mattered to them but an antique ghost,
And the open rent in their sides it cackled through.
One can imagine what sly words they said
To shrug the violence off and half explain
A foundered world, then pack her off to bed;
Speed was what counted, they'd to fight again
Within a ring they tried to think their own-
Making the darkness where she lay alone.

Such smilings, though, on the morning after that night!
Red-handed both of them, they groped for chat-
It's easy to make darkness but not light-
He pointed out the business of some cat,

There on the lawn, the feathers of a bird,
But knew she knew the game that they'd been at:
Those burnt out eyes of her had never stirred
From what between them in the night occurred.

'A door,' he murmured, 'a door bruised mother's eye?'
She stared of course clean through that question mark,
Puzzled he'd offered her a half-baked lie.
Like cats, he thought, a child sees through the dark,
And, with no adult technique of escape,
Runs the bad gauntlet of its parents' dream:
What is a fitting panacea for rape?
Strawberries I think they offered and whipped cream;
Within that garden where the shapes of night
Still prowled about them in the June sunlight.

As bedtime came, he sensed her terror grow;
Would it rise again, the petroleum sea, and pluck
Their features away in its savage undertow;
Must she ride their beaten minds down gulfs of shock?
She undergoes, he thought, what we've undergone-
Remembering, himself a child, how the house would rock-

Will this circle of revenants never, never be done,
Must ever the haunted ones to haunt come back?
He turned and saw his daughter was asleep,
His wife beside her in the faint blue air;
It seems as well as furies of the deep,
Moments of clarity we also share.
Leeds 1957

A Smell of Burning

After each savage, hysterical episode,
So common with us, my mother would sniff the air
And murmur, 'Nurse, would you look at the upstairs fire.
I smell burning, something's alight somewhere.'
But a red coal never was found, or jet of gas,

Scorching dry board, or paint-work beginning to melt;
And too young was I in that nursery time to guess
What smoking, subjective fire she really smelt.

Nowadays I know quite well from hers they came,
And my father's mouth, when the hot tongues crackled and spat;
But what mattered then was a trick of dodging flame,
And keeping some breath alive in the heat of it.
I have it still that inbred dodging trick;
But always - when fire beset - I see them turning,
My parents, to name elsewhere their sour fire reak,
And touch myself and know what's really burning.

Orpheus and Eurydice

I think he was mistaken all the while,
This singer, who believed love rinsed away
With all its flowering murmurs and green leaves,
Through the black crevice of a dying day.
It's true that she gave up before he needed
The habits of her blood and gusty breath,
But if he could have seen how brief the journey
That held him from her country and his death,
Love would have stayed itself, and not been caught in
The white-eyed moment when she turned to stone;
So he'd have seen, beyond a perished station,
The occasion other dying was his own.

Perhaps it was his death that he drew back from;
I mean, that like a page he dared not turn,
He'd pored too long upon his own black letters;
It he had struck a match and let them burn,
Nor here nor there at all, without a substance,
Or any circumstance, he might have found
His wife was omnipresent as his nature,
And not have sought her shadow underground.

Almost he understood one bitter evening
That Eurydice was not here or there,
And walked away half smiling from her tombstone,
As if he breathed her in the general air.
But emptiness grew large and whimpered round him.
He fumbled for the light; he touched her dress.
Now as that haunted velvet ferries back
The memory of her blood and nakedness,
And he turns round from their uncreatured marriage

To seek her body, there, among the graves,
I hear the dog-teeth in the outer darkness,
A plunging, seaborne head that moans and raves.

A Small Keen Wind

My wife for six months now in sinister
Tones has muttered incessantly about divorce,
And, since of the woman I'm fond, this dark chatter
Is painful as well as a bit monotonous.
Still, marvel one must, when she fishes out of that trunk,
Like rags, my shadier deeds for all to see
With 'This you did when sober, and that when drunk',
At the remarkable powers of memory.
For although I wriggle like mad when she whistles up
Some particularly nasty bit of handiwork
The dirty linen I simply cannot drop,
Since 'Thomas Blackburn' is stitched by the laundry mark.
So I gather the things and say, 'Yes, these are mine,
Though some cleaner items are not upon your list',
Then walk with my bundle of rags to another room
Since I will not play the role of delinquent ghost
And be folded up by guilt in the crook of an arm.
I saw tonight - walking to cool the mind -
A little moonshine on a garden wall
And, as I brooded, felt a small, keen wind
Stroll from the Arctic at its own sweet will.

JANE BLUETT

2 am
Nobody's ugly after 2am - **Charles Bukowski**

1.

An arm bruised, puffed like so much meat,
swings to a cleaver rhythm
this suicidal Saturday.
She drinks in dust and decay
through gyrating human debris
seeps from one track to the next
catches eyes - collects them for later.
Walking home she slurs
through littered streets
remembers the old man with the baby
the way ambulances move through traffic.
She smiles.

2.

The theatrical toad slips tonic to his gin
swills in the drinkers den
Camp sycophants bow, leave
scraping eyes with him
to be spat out later in bitter wit.
"I was once in bar with Burton.."
We were all in bars with someone
waiting for entrance, open door
closing encore.
He is grounded - sees the girl laugh at the bar
and thinks of the slow removal of flesh.
He smiles but his teeth are yellow.

3.

I love you at midnight
like the Chinese State Circus in Nottingham,
the schoolboy carrying his bag,
the pensioner seducing his wife.
The future is a furrow in my stomach.

Tomorrow is a warm bath, soft towels.
But you turn your eyes -
take them to women whose names are silent.
Love after hours is the face of the small child
at a zebra crossing
staring at traffic.

4.

An arm outstretched, in tight silence
welcomes union with sharp untainted steel.
His mistress spits through throbbing flesh
headstrong on a stained green mattress,
Communion is metal confidential
as the arm bends with a sigh outstretched to the laughing skin.
Love tonight is amnesiac blue
smells of whiskey and cigarettes
and burned spoons.
Foul fragrance leads his patchwork friends
to a green mattress where the stain of his face
smiles.

5.

Anthony in green velvet carries his horse to bed
to slay dragons.
His mother has wished him away
now in sleep he disappears.
He tears through school books
of fat freckled rejection
drowns in Brecht, Bukowski and better offers.
"It is pointless to build a well," he thinks
"on concrete
and unfed babies invariably die."
The clock smiles.

EDWIN BROCK

When My Father Died

On the day my father died
    all the hoops in the neighbourhood rang
    skate wheels shrilled on summer pavements
    and I in my blakey-boots clanged one foot
    in each gutter

On the day my father died
    girls were running autumn-eyed, with wild hair
    and hands of silk; peg-tops had come round again
    and in the sky the angels were as plain as wings

But on the day my father died
    white faces fell from every window
    and every house found rooms of tears to hide
    while I, joy-jumping, empty-eyed sang on the day
    my father died

Now my father dies a little every day
And the faces from each window grow like mine.

An Attempt at Exorcism

Now it is your yellow dress and young
sun-coloured legs that I remember
and the Old Bridge in Dulwich Park
and the ducks being noisy about summer
and this, though false, is something which persists
like the jammed note of a car-horn in
a long and lonely street, and the one and only
memory of drowning, which also is untrue.

For now I can no longer shuffle you
from memory, but turn up Jokers in my hand
along with Kings and Queens. Of course
there may have been no yellow dress

and the Old Bridge, which is now made
of stone, is also suspect. Perhaps

only ducks, then, and their noisy summers
still exist; that and your yellow-coloured legs.

In Memory of My Grandmother

That morning my grandmother came down
to the hearth and laid sticks and paper
outside the stove; lighting them, she sat
warming her plump and gentle hands and
watched the kitchen fill with smoke; until
my grandfather, between his garden flowers,
called her a stupid cow and a doctor who
ordered her to bed, where she died.

My grandmother's death caused more weeping
than a drowned cat. All the family wept
from room to room, but nobody recalled
that she had lit her fire outside its
black accustomed prison, nor that
she had sat entranced by flames before
the doctor and the smoke dragged her away.

Nobody said any more than that she died;
and, of course, the family wore black;
yet I can very easily see the way
a strong desire to free all fire could
capture her, and that the thought of
doctors or of dying would not occur.

Perhaps it was the knowledge that the fire
would be extinguished finished her. And
that nobody in the smoke-filled room had seen
that all the flames had started in her eyes.

A Clutter of Mothers

Many-clothed and smelling of cheap soap
are all the mothers I have known;
many-mouthed, loudly critical and alone.

Not often pregnant, they appear always
in a horde of children begging at
sweet-counters; not often rich, they swear

that every mouthful is the last. I have loved
all mothers from time to time: mother
Church, mother Hubbard and poor old

mother Brock, yet I will never understand
why every woman taking my dumb hand
between her own remains so true to type:

many-mouthed, loudly critical, alone,
declaring that the best is always past
and swearing that each mouthful is my last.

The Curtain Poem

A home should have a wife, a cat
and blinds upon the windows that
when pulled aside are suddenly drawn back
again. A wife should have a cat to kick

a home to love and, if I have not made
my meaning plain, a curtain to be drawn
aside and suddenly pulled back again.

A man should have a wife to love
a home to kick and cats upon the curtains which
he may from time to time refrain
from seizing to and back again.

But if a home should have a man
who waits upon a window-sill
endeavouring to find a plan
for all that moves outside the pane

be sure the home will have a wife
perhaps the wife will have a cat
but if by now my meaning is not plain
the wife in all her mystery should
turn her back upon the scream
and, singing, seize the cloth across again.

Five Ways to Kill a Man

There are many cumbersome ways to kill a man:
you can make him carry a plank of wood
to the top of a hill and nail him to it. To do this
properly you require a crowd of people
wearing sandals, a cock that crows, a cloak
to dissect, a sponge, some vinegar and one
man to hammer the nails home.

Or you can take a length of steel,
shaped and chased in a traditional way,
and attempt to pierce the metal cage he wears.
But for this you need white horses,
English trees, men with bows and arrows,
at least two flags, a prince and
a castle to hold your banquet in.

Dispensing with nobility, you may, if the wind
allows, blow gas at him. But then you need
a mile of mud sliced through with ditches,
not to mention black boots, bomb craters,
more mud, a plague of rats, a dozen songs
and some round hats made of steel.
In an age of aeroplanes, you may fly
miles above your victim and dispose of him by
pressing one small switch. All you then
require is an ocean to separate you, two
systems of government, a nation's scientists,
several factories, a psychopath and
land that no one needs for several years.

These are, as I began, cumbersome ways
to kill a man. Simpler, direct, and much more neat
is to see that he is living somewhere in the middle
of the twentieth century, and leave him there.

A Moment of Respect

Two things I remember about my grandfather:
his threadbare trousers, and the way he adjusted
his half-hunter watch two minutes every day.

When I asked him why he needed to know the time so
exactly, he said a business man could lose a fortune
by being two minutes late for an appointment.

When he died he left two meerschaum pipes
and a golden sovereign on a chain. Somebody
threw the meerschaum pipes away, and
there was an argument about the sovereign.

On the day of his burial the church clock chimed
as he was lowered down into the clay, and all
the family advanced their watches by two minutes.

Unlucky Jim

My father was a man who laughed at charms
Walked under ladders and whistled at the wind
Who would not turn his silver at the moon's command
Nor cross his breast when freed from mortal sin.

My father was a man among all men
Threw bullseye darts in grinning public bars
Who seven-nightly at the call of ten
Would hang his paper hat upon the stars.

And daily I have seen my mother sit
With knives uncrossed beside a silver gnome
Polishing St Christopher with salt and spit
To hold the wind that hauls the traveller home.

But all the luck in all the lonely world
And all the double-darts and wringing hands
Were far away the day my father died
Or saw him fall and would not understand.

JOHN BUTTERWORTH

To my Ideal Lady
(mystic love for an ideal woman)

You are sweeter the sweetest maiden,
As sweet, indeed, as the fragrance
Of the flowers picked from the fields of Heaven.
I cannot help but be in love with you
Who are so sweet, maternal and full of pure tenderness.
Inspired am I as my spine tingles with ecstasy
Sensing the aura of your loveliness
Which is more beautiful than the music of the spheres.

What tenderness can you imagine that I would bestow
With all my devotion on your body and soul?
Let me take you by your serenest hand, trembling,
And wipe away any tears from your face with the utmost sympathy
Great star that shines so bright and so well.
Magnificent you are fair loved grace
Who seeks to relieve the misery of others
Most magnanimously with expert career and concern.

It is my wish that you live in paradise,
Let the bird of paradise fly over and court you
Immortal Beloved on whom all beauty shines!
You are my life's great dream, the magical secret of happiness.
In you one would find it, a much sweeter elixir of life
So much better than the alchemist's dream of gold
And far better than all the wealth of the world
You are a joy to all those who you love!
If you want to know what I have seen in you, think of you,
It is written in the world's greatest music, my love
Without all that you and the world would not be complete.
Would to God that we could create great beauty,
But if I did this, it would be nowhere near as good as yours
Serenest Lady, to whom my soul aspires!
Never will I fall short of your affection, or abuse you
My angel, my Heaven, my most exalted sweet love!

Dedicated to the Starving

On your hands should be sapphires,
Your eating plates should be made of gold
And you should eat the very best food, plentiful,
That tastes just like manna from Heaven
As the stone that the builders rejected has become
The main cornerstone, so a city of the most costly marble
Should be built for you, all you starving ones
Who would have perished by the rich world's greed.
Indeed the rich world has had an innings
But now it is your turn, you the cheated ones
To be privileged and to rule:-
Do this peacefully and you deserve the promised land.

May your sheep and cattle flood the markets,
Your bounteous banquet soar like a mountain
And a lasting peace, surpassing all understanding
Light up and fill your valleys.
Daughters of Africa, may you be prepared to meet
Your bridegrooms in a land of plenty.
May their service be magnificent,
May their devotion and yours be profound
And your happiness be magnified many times!
Let the children of Africa be given hope and courage
To build all these things for their country and for all.
All do this for the benefit of all, and you should win the promised land.

Invitation to Natural Beauty

Let's see the beautiful sky on star- lit nights,
Let's go up far north to see the Northern Lights:-
Colour majestic, of the cold climate, ornate.
Let's climb the Skirrid mountain's summit straight
See winter snowdrops, crocuses in spring
Narcissi, daffodils, the ice will sing
And notice new born lambs in pleasant pastures
Do rouse the joys of spring as life matures

See flames of methane gas near fetid marshes;
See cumulus clouds so typical of Marches.
Let's see the eel oft rippling in the river;

Observe the glowworm's luminous skin's silver,
See frosted patterns etched on window panes:-
There're poems on these inspired from astral planes.
See stalagmites and stalactites in caves
Whose elements which the potholer braves.

Let's visit lakes where swans stand dignified,
By Nature's beauty so well fortified
And hear the thunder, see the lightening flashes,
The roll of the ocean and shores which it lashes.
See birds in courtship like displays of peacocks
With feathers right outstretched. See doves in flocks.
Pursue the contemplation of all Nature,
The beauty grand from God for us to nurture.
Let's hear the silent music of the summer
In mellow mood with breezes mild and warmer
Observe the autumn leaves so colourful
An Heraclitean Fire most beautiful!
Let's see the grand and graceful golden sunset
The Heaven's jewel on our horizon set.
Perceive the rainbow of the waterfall:
Eternity in Nature, all in all!

IDRIS CAFFREY

White Room

The hay will not wait
another day to be cut -
the snow not lie
in the winding lanes
until the children come.

It is we who wait -
wait for the room
to fill with flowers,
night to cover a sun
still finding ways to stay.

Getting Through

Always against the odds,
the bird with the broken wing,
the toy boat bobbing
down the estuary
finding its way to the sea.

Getting through -
perhaps that's all we can ever do
and just sometimes, an evening sky
telling us that tomorrow
will be a glorious day.

MARGARET THERESA CARNEY

Alice Living in the Looking Glass

She thought she met a caterpillar:
On his mushroom he laughed,
Idle and drugged -
Offered her a different medication -
His attitude enlarged her paranoia,
It did not help the situation.
O Alice.
It had begun by looking in the glass,
To scan the future, or rinse her soul pure.
Schizophrenia kept her there -
Halluciogenically challenged.
A cake said, or was it a bottle?
Eat and drink them
Big and small not there at all
Flying from her head
She listened to what the voices said
O Alice
In memories are you existing?
In what dreaming time live you?
Friends and relations spin, and pause
Psychoanalysis looks for the cause.
Alice is happier, and happier
Surely it's not so bad,
To have gone irrevocably mad.
Alice, sedated, giggles and curses
Marching around are the psychiatric nurses,
'Sick in the head' people say,
Alice kneels to pray.
'Real Life' seems so dull,
Now her mind is full; -
Unicorns dance across her sight
Elves, hobgoblins - fantasy such
As would fill a story book.
Alice, O Alice
Living in The Looking Glass.
She got better, worked in a shop
One day she heard a little hop ...
... The White Rabbit - full-blown,

Came back to take Alice home.
Demented, fragmented
All Alone with her visions.
Alice felt she could fly
Inside the Looking Glass -
Safe, no evil could pass.
All her selves lined up,
Her personality split.
Turned her crystal slipper
On a glass stair,
Climbed into the mirror,
Quiet now, and calm
Alice could no more
Come to any harm.

Reflections

I think that at the beginning,
Of madness I was very small.
Small and lost in a paranoid world.
The voices taunted me and people mocked.
Oh I saw them all, all the people in the white suits.
I ranged the highway lost inside myself.
Reality did not seem real, it was too hard.
I spent Christmas in an institution.
We drank tea and we were casualties
Accidents of life, a death, an illness
Loneliness the Lavender lace of solitude.
I tried to reach out but there was a screen,
A screen of broken images
Silhouettes and Flashes, illusion, illusion,
Memories and fantasies all overgrown.
Dad says I get by,
They have stopped putting me away,
I moved and I got a little house.
And I fought like a tigress
To keep it together.
The mind can be a terrible thing,
Untethered, let free.
But at last I did love myself,
I did finally love myself,
And I stood alone, on a great dark cliff

And I called the wild dark seas
I called them to my breast.
I am a poet
And the words fell like blood drops
From a large soul.

ANGELA CARTER

My Cat in Her First Spring

With the spring coming, my cat is beginning to bud.
sprouting nipples all along her long, white breast.
this long-legged, adolescent she.

And in the strange
country fitfully lit by the inward-turning suns
    of her yellow
eyes, such alien trees shake out moist leaf
and the seed-crusted ferns uncoil with a slow blindness
in the rich fruit-cake of her dark recesses
    where the wrinkled
intuitions of her summer roses stir and tremble
    in their sleep
for spring is coming, and the fat buds bulge.

Life-affirming Poem
about Small Pregnant White Cat

She sits (slumps); and-she-bulging sack of life-
    becomes a
melting snow-cat haphazardly thrown together
by careless children. Stuffed full,

brim-full

FULL

(to the teeth)
with kittens, she yowls-and you fear an incontinent
brindled kindle will burst wrong ways, out of the pink
Front door.
Inside the swollen sides of the small white cat
(who suddenly, unexpectedly, finds herself so heavy she
thumps about, clattering) snugly
buttoned under two pink ranks of nipples
(such an ermine and double-breasted jacket she wears
as used by

Shirley Temple (such an ingénue is she, was she but now
betrayed)
buttoned up inside her-inside (conceive!)

that taut stretched womb, crammed-some more
than base Indian black hole (is it, in there, is it like
a slit capsicum, clutch of seed hugging
the central column of an inexpressible convoluted
interior? is it like that?)

regardless-(Miracle of Everyday Things)-inside her
all the little furry commas lie blindly,
    futurity in futurity
stirring shifting waiting
    to be born

The Horse of Love

The colour of the round moon is yellow, yellow
as lemons (old lemon slice moon) tumbling in
        dark leaves.
Sharp, clean and pleasing yellow; and
this is the land where the lemon trees grow.

The Horse of Love jumps over the moon, sharing
out blue mythopaeic dust from mane, from tail.
from fringed anemone eyes.
Horse (of Love) bearing
this clasped, amorous couple. Their faces, sharing
a profile, merging; the small
soft hands of the wind twining and plaiting
streamers of hair.

        And any fool knows
forepart, hindquarters, formed of two lovers
        (Horse of Love)
huddled under the hide (moths in the crutch)
slapstick old horse

not fit for daytime, only for night, for concealing dark, this
garish old horse, ragged old horse,
patchwork of skin of the mother-in-law that bit you
      dishcloths
        facecloths,
contraceptives, gas bills, curlers, pimples, body odour.
face cream, stained vests, sanitary towels skulking
rat-like under beds full of no rose petals but crumbs
of last night's fish-paste sandwiches and the fecund
milk bottles breeding under the sink
etc. etc.. etc

YET:

'Yes, see-we
climb high on this pantomime horse
so squeeze the moon into our tea
and spread (green cheese) the moon on our bread.'

Poem for a Wedding Photograph

Posing for the photographer,
they stand together under a green tree
in bridal and unfamiliar clothes.
Dressed up, they are strangers to one another.
They move awkwardly, smile
the shy, nervous smiles of shipwrecked voyagers,
never met on the crowded liner till now, in the
    open boat,
embarking in embarrassment on a strange voyage,
    together,
over a strange sea. Improvise
a sail from all her satin, make a mast
out of his body. Their hands clutch, suddenly.
We have only each other. Who are we?

Under the green tree, the bride,
gift-wrapped in white. Her veil drifts in the wind,
caressing his good black suit. The shutter clicks.
They are taken. Frozen in this eternal moment,
    forever.
Scissored out of the fabric of their time.
an icon of marriage (like Arnolfini and his wife
in the cluttered room. with the little dog,
to signify fidelity).

In the garden, under a tree,
the first man and wife of all and ever,
in a silver frame, for life.

Poem for Robinson Crusoe

Such a vile beach. Dandruff sand creaks underfoot.
    shifting:
the dark tide of the unmapped black sea called
    'Lack-of-Love'
surges (with the motion of vomiting)
sicking up its detritus all over the shore;
these bones of dead vessels grown all over
    (obscene fungus)
with used contraceptives, slimy mementoes
of life affirming impulses which never quite made
    never quite
    never made it;
multiple-fractured limbs of the chair the impossible girl
curled impregnably in; hospital beds, ocean gone,
bleeding rust;
crepe bandages unfurl slowly along the water
    ectoplasm
heraldically breast-plated with dented cans,
    storm-tossed sailors,
blanched by water, loll among sewage; their eyes
have been put out by pearls; mackerels
ate their fingers, genitals, toes, noses.

Among such leering images of romantic decay. Crusoe
judged that the best thing to do was to make
    a shielding
parasol against the tropic sun; then.
cannily stuffing his pockets with pearls (blind to the
empty eyeholes agape like hell's mouse runs), he
turns inland. He puts his back to the black sea
and all its symbolic refuse.
He teased sweet milk from the at-first unwilling goat.
Constructed useful pots. Dried
for raisins the hitherto Dionysiac grape (for a
    spotted dog
in the wilderness is man's best friend).
And-final triumph of man over environment-
    he taught

the lacquered flocks of parrots (acrobatic
tea trays at an evening party where he was the
   only guest)
to remind him of his identity ('Robin Crusoe!')
and hoarsely to mock his self-pity ('Poor
Robin Crusoe !')
and thus he alienated his self-pity
after the manner of Brecht.

Shortly the wilderness shook out golden flowers,
the black sea bobbed with water-lilies,
and Crusoe sang, on Sundays, metrical versions
   of the psalms.

KEN CHAMPION

Things

Gaps in cupboards
spaces in wardrobes
sitting on the stair
he knows she's gone.

The ornaments remain,
Wedgwood, Llandro figurines,
Regency beaus, flower sellers
a girl with a cake teasing a dog
two children in a nursery fight
one holding a pillow above her head.

He places them on the floor,
a sheep standing in a saucer
an owl upside down in a bowl
lovers in an armless embrace
the new stumps strangely aged
gathers handfuls, armfuls, sackfuls
lays them in a line in the hall,
treads on the protruding spout
of an elephant teapot.

DEBJANI CHATTERJEE

On a Midland Mainline Train

"It is your God speaking...."
The tannoy boomed its Sheffield welcome.
I sat up with a jolt – derailed.
"Good God!" I said, and looked around.
Anonymous passengers smiled broadly.
Sheepishly, I added: "at least we're in good hands."

The Midland Mainlines train left Chesterfield.
Its legendary steeple, witchery-twisted,
receded into an anonymous soothing blur.
'Trailing clouds of glory' haloed
England's miles of pleasant green.

As we left Derby, the miracle play resumed.
The immigrant voice hosannaad on the intercom
to grinning polytheists, pagans, sinners, saints....
No compromise, we were all addressed by none other
than our equal opportunities Deity.

"It is your God speaking," chanted the litany
as we pulled out of multilingual Leicester.
Swagatam and *Bien venue*, *Khuda hafiz* and goodbye....
And then the astonishing denouement: our God apologised
for an act of God that had made us eight minutes late!

Ruffled Feathers

My parrot with the ruffled feathers
is bolshie;
its language
is nobody's business;
its squawk stabs the ears.

And such attitude!
You see it when it cocks its head;
catch its crazed gleam - and freeze!
When it flies
above you - duck!

My bird's one wicked pet.
Yeah - it's teaching me a thing or two.

Hospital View
(Dacca Medical College, 1960)

Clutching veranda rails, she watched the ground.
Eyes mesmerised, head spinning round and round.

His *lungi* folded above bony knees,
The barefoot man was circling round and round.

Terror swamped her typhoid room; cleaver raised,
He chased a chicken squawking round and round.

The bird ran helter-skelter, bead eyes glazed
At heaven's square, walls closing round and round.

Dizzied by the desperate dance below,
She stumbled, her eyes racing round and round.

The sedated sky promised no escape,
Headless bird and man reeling round and round.

Along lime-washed white walls, she dragged herself,
The antiseptic reeking round and round.

Starched sheet jagged against her chin, she curled;
Debjani's stomach heaving round and round.

Marilyn

Marilyn Monroe
had the sense to know
that the wind, and the whole world, waited
for her skirt to blow.

A ghazal by Debjani Chatterjee

He was born of a second wife, the second son,
but the sweetness of his verse was second to none.

'Hold love true,' his dervish father said, 'Love is all.'
Poor though he was, his riches were second to none.

Heart-broken, he saw love's cruel face in the moon.
In young romance, his madness smiled second to none.

His love was bountiful beauty, pure poetry,
one divinity; his love was second to none.

Hindus and Muslims honoured their poet of love.
Love was his nature, his greatness second to none.

Agra-born, Delhi-made, Lucknow cradles his bones.
All share and own the one who was second to none.

Foremost of poets, Mir was first among lovers.
Love was his language, his words sing second to none.

This is a ghazal in honour of the Urdu poet Mohammad Taqi Mir (1723-1810), who was born in Agra, the city of that great monument to love – the Taj Mahal, and died in Lucknow. His autobiography states that he was educated by his dervish father who advised him to make love his goal in life. As an adolescent in Delhi, Mir suffered a mental breakdown and was haunted by a face in the moon. Mir survived a period of very sadistic treatment, and started writing. He became a much-loved poet, patronised by both Hindu and Muslim nobility. He died in Lucknow. A great Romantic poet, Mir was a profound influence on the Urdu poets who followed him.

2 Songs by Kazi Nazrul Islam
Translated from Bengali by Debjani Chatterjee

I've Ink on my Hands

Oh Mother, I've ink on my hands and on my face!
Looking at my inky face, the neighbours just laugh.
Since I haven't any learning, Mother, I see
only my dark Mother when I view the letter 'M'.
When I see the letter 'K' I call out 'Kali'
and I dance to the clapping of my hands.
When I see the black multiplication signs, Mother,
it is only my tears that multiply in streams.
I could never learn the alphabet of colours

since your dark shade was not among them, Mother.
But all that you write on forest leaves, sea-water,
the sky's book – that's writing I can certainly read.
So what if people label me 'illiterate'!

Note: This is a song to Kali. In the Bengali original there is a pun on the word Kali, which is not only the name of a goddess, but also means 'ink' and 'black'.

The Eid Moon

O spiritual guide, say where does God's Messenger reside?
What must I do to see him? Where should I go?
His seat is in faraway Heaven by God's side.
He is so dear that God keeps him hidden near Him.
I read the *Quran*, I listen to the *Hadith*, but they don't satisfy.
Having smelt its perfume, my heart wants to see the flower.
All rejoice to sight the new moon of Eid, so why does my soul cry?
When will I see Mustafa? *He* is the Eid moon to me.

Note: Mustafa is another name for Mohammed.

3 Poems by Kazi Nazrul Islam
Translated from Bengali by Debjani Chatterjee

The Rebel

    O rebel-hero, speak.
  Say: I tower over the highest peak!
In my presence the snow-topped mountain bows its head!

    O rebel-hero, speak.
  Say: I tear the fabric of the universe,
    I outrun the moon, the sun, the planets and the stars.
    Beyond the throne of God Himself
    I rise, a perpetual wonder!
I am the lustre of victory on the sun-god's brow!
    O rebel-hero, speak.
  Say: I tower over the highest peak!

I am untamable, savage indomitable,
  the bringer of apocalypse, the cyclone's fury, I am annihilation!

The ultimate terror, I am the curse of the Earth,
I am inevitable, irresistible,
I crush all, I destroy everything!
I recognise no constraints,
break all ties, know no bondage of rules!
I obey no laws,
I drown the loaded boats, I am a torpedo, a volcanic mine!
I am Shiva at the end of time, the sudden shock of summer storms,
I am a rebel, born of a rebel - I am invincible!
O rebel-hero, speak.
Say: I tower over the highest peak!

I am a hurricane and a tornado,
I demolish all that I find in my way!
I am in the delirium of the dancer's drum;
dancing to my own rhythm, I am life's exhilarating freedom.
I am melody, euphony and symphony;
life's restless vivacity and sparkle,
the sudden marvel that one meets along the way,
I trigger the leaping spring in one's step!
I am the enticing invigorating pulse of music!
Brother, I do whatever whenever my spirit urges:
I embrace my foe, I arm-wrestle with death,
I am insane, I am turmoil!
I am the great pestilence, this earth's dreaded terror.
Nemesis of tyranny, I am justice; I burn with an ever restless flame.
O rebel-hero, speak.
Say: I tower over the highest peak!

Forever impassioned, I am irrepressible;
my life's cup is ever full to the brim and overflowing!
I am the flame of sacrifice and its divine guardian,
I am the sacrifice and the priest, I am fire itself!
I am creation and destruction, the dwelling and the cremation ground.
I am the end and also the end of the night!
I am Indrani's son, the moon sits in my hand and the sun on my brow.
My one hand holds a melodious bamboo flute, the other a bugle of battle.
I am the 'blue-throated', poisoned when drinking from the ocean of pain!
I am Bomkesh and hold the free-flowing Ganges in my matted locks.
O rebel-hero, speak.
Say: I tower over the highest peak!

I am an ascetic sage and musician.
I am a prince; my royal attire is of dullest saffron.
I am a Bedouin, I am Chengis.
I salute none but myself.
I am thunder; I am the sound of *OM* in Ishan's conch.
I am the mighty call of Israfil's trumpet;
I am Pinakapani's hand-drum and trident,
the sceptre of Dharma, God of Justice.
I am the *chakra* and the mighty conch,
I am the tremendous primeval sound.
I am Durbasha, Vishwamitra's furious pupil.
I am a raging fire that will burn down the earth!
I am the unbridled laughter that petrifies creation,
I am the eclipse of a dozen suns on Doomsday.
Sometimes serene and sometimes frantic, I am most wilful.
I am the new blood of youth; I humble the pride of Destiny!
I am the tempest's raging wind, the ocean's thunderous roar.
I am luminous and resplendent.
I am the lap-lapping and slapping of water,
the rhythmic music of waves!

I am the maiden's free-flowing hair, the sparkle in her eyes.
I am sweet sixteen's first blossoming love, I am bliss itself!
I am the distressed mind of the despondent,
I am the widow's mournful sigh, the torment of those without hope.
I am the misery of all who are homeless,
the pounding pain of the mortified,
poison's sting and the lovelorn heart's distress.
Ever-proud and disappointed, my mind wells in an agony of despair.
I am the virgin's first hesitant kiss!
I am a moment's fleeting look,
the sidelong glance of the clandestine lover;
I am the love of a restless maid, the tinkling of her bangles!
I am the eternal child, the eternal youth,
I am the modesty and restraint of the country maid.
I am the North Wind, blowing about; and the careless eastern breeze.
I am the street minstrel's ballad, his flute, his lute and song!
I am the unquenched thirst of summer, the sun's blazing blistering heat,
I am a gently flowing desert brook, and the green and shaded oasis!
I run in wild abandon; what madness is this? I am insane!
Of a sudden I have recognised myself, all my blinkers are shed!
I am the rise and also the fall, awareness in the unconscious mind,

I am Victory's banner, humanity's triumphant call.
Tempestuous, I rush through Heaven and Earth;
the great Borrak and Uchchaishraba are my mounts,
    neighing like thunder!
In the earth's bosom I am an erupting volcano,
a fiery ocean below the earth.
Sitting astride lightning, I click my fingers and leap,
spreading panic and upheaval with fiery earthquakes.
I grab the Serpent Vasuki's hood,
I clutch the blazing wing of Heaven's Messenger Gibrail!
I am the divine child, mischievous and unruly:
with my teeth I tear Mother Earth's sari-cloth!

I am the flute of Orpheus,
I lull the heaving ocean;
the kiss of my music soothes
the restless world to sleep!
I am the flute in Shyama's hands.
When I traverse the skies in fury,
the fires of seven hells and of *Habia*, the most hellish hell,
flicker in fear and are extinguished.
I am the rebel-messenger on earth and in the sky.
I am a mighty monsoon flood:
sometimes I am a blessing to the earth,
sometimes a devastating curse.
I will tear away the twin maids from Vishnu's chest!
I am oppression, I am a meteor and I am Saturn;
a fiery comet, a venomous cobra!
I am beheaded Chandi, the destroyer Ranada.
Seated in the fires of hell, I laugh the laughter of a flower.
I am composed of both earth and spirit,
resolute and immortal, I am imperishable, immutable.
    The scourge of humans, gods and demons,
      I am disaster for all eternity.
      I am the truth at the core of divinity.
I roam where I will on Heaven, Earth and Hell,
    all fury let loose, I am insane, insane!
Today I know myself; I have broken every chain!
    I am the terrible axe of Parashurama
and will rid the world of warriors to wrest a perfect peace!
    I am the mighty plough of Balarama
and will smite the tyrant to furrow a new world cycle.

   Battle-weary, I am the arch rebel of life.
   I will not rest, I must engage in constant strife.
I will not have the screams of the oppressed rend the air,
I will not have the Earth cry out from the tyrant's sword.
   Battle-weary, I am the arch rebel of life.
   I will not rest, I must engage in constant strife.

Rebel on a precipice: I plant my footprints on God's chest,
I challenge the despot; I will rip out the fickle heart of Fate!
Rebel on a precipice: I will plant my footprints on God's chest,

     I will rip out the fickle heart of Fate!
Alone I stand, in the wide world I tower.
I am unvanquished, an arch rebel forever.

Hope

   Perhaps I will have sight of you
where the sky bows its head to kiss the forest's green-edged hue.

    In this far distant village field,
    on raised dust-paths or lonely banks,
    perhaps you will come and, smiling
      playfully, hold me by my hand.

Without a veil, you glance at me across this blue expanse.
This southern breeze is the horizon's secret messenger.

    From in between the forest trees,
    you come to kiss my eyes and tease.
    This is the only thing, behold,
      etched on the sky in lines of gold!

Conqueror

O my queen, I finally recognise defeat.
My vanquished banner lies trampled beneath your feet.

My immortal sword has always won victory,
but grows weary day by day - it is grown heavy.
Let me lose this burden now and give it to you.

Let me crown your hair with this wreath of my defeat.

O Goddess of Life! Why look at me and shed tears
to make the monuments of victors quake with fear?

Today at the helm of this rebel's bloodied chariot,
Conqueror, the end of your blue sari flutters.
I have woven all my weapons into your garland.
Drowned in tears, I emerge in triumph from defeat.

Kazi Nazrul Islam (1899-1976) was a great Indian writer and Bangladesh's national poet. He endured great poverty in childhood and had little formal education. He is called 'the rebel poet' after his most famous poem. Opposed to British rule in India, he was jailed for his writings. A Muslim married to a Hindu, Nazrul was passionately committed to Hindu-Muslim solidarity. He wrote many Hindu and Muslim devotional songs, as well as love lyrics, ghazals and protest poems. He fell ill in 1942 and spent time in mental hospitals. For the remainder of his life he never spoke. Debjani Chatterjee produced a Nazrul poster-poem pack for Survivors' Poetry, which was published in 2001. Two of the posters contained short extracts from 'The Rebel', so we are pleased to now publish Debjani's translation of this famous poem in its entirety.

KEVIN CROSSLEY-HOLLAND

A Dream of a Meeting

Rooted I watch, watch the girl
approach in a street hedged with
poppies, trembling, hollyhocks
nodding their acquiescence.
There are always hollyhocks.
Gravely she walks with perfect
equilibrium; daylight
sleepwalker, ashen-faced,
she looms towards this meeting
she knows nothing of.
                    I strain
my eyes to see her features
as a sculptor searches stone,
finding there correlatives
of his own huge passion.
Her face is a lily spathe
with no blemish, and her hair,
moon-pale, falls out behind her.
Green-sheathed she grows now, grows
towards me.
          And then I see
she is only eight, maybe
nine. A cigarette, unlit,
waits in her mouth. Still rooted,
I frown like the puritan
I am, I still partly am.
No, not a cigarette, no,
it is a thermometer
jammed under her tongue; the sun
angles off it.
            And she comes
so very close now, at last
she sees me, hands outstretched.
Her eyes are child's marbles
as she gives me the slender,
gleaming stem of glass, passes
by me; and she does not even
change her metronomic pace.

The sap surges within me,
I look for the mercury:
it is all, all in the bulb,
in the bulb this summer day.
Rooted, I ache. And the girl
goes on gravely. Unknowing,
she brushes trembling poppies
with her bare legs; their scarlet
petals spill like drops of blood.
And all the hollyhocks nod.

The Wall

I am a desolate wall, accumulator of lichen.
Men made me with flint chippings and, fickle as always,
ignored me; time did not ignore them.
My business is to divide things: the green ribbons
of grass from the streams of macadam; the kitchen gardens
from the marsh acres, garish with sea-lavender;
the copses of ilex and pine from the North Sea,
the bludgeoning waves of salt water where seabirds play.
I stand grey under the East Anglian sky,
glint when the occasional sun opens its eye.
My business is to divide things, my duty to protect.
I am unrepaired; men neglect me at their own risk.
Time takes me in mouthfuls; the teeth of the frost
bit into my body here; here my mortar crumbles;
the wind rubs salt into every wound.
Elsewhere I am overgrown with insidious ivy;
it wound its arms around me only to strangle me.

Relentless, the sea rolls down from the Pole.
It levelled the dunes last year, removed the marram grass,
clashed its steel cymbals over the marsh and macadam.
It attacked me and undermined me; I sway
like a drunkard now; yet it could not gash me
with its gleaming scythes; it was not strong enough.
I stand, sad, and stare at all this estate,
the lawns, the kitchen gardens, copses garrulous
in the wind. I carefully listen, listen and wait
for the fierce outsider to force his way in.

Confessional

I come once more to this terrible place;
As it was it is, each stone and each face

Unchanged, making an index of the change
In me. Everything here was arranged

Long ago; the wind, raking from the north,
Saw to that and sees to it. In the hearth

Coals glow and the ash flies early and late;
Every face is ruckled, sands corrugate;

Inland, those superstitious hawthorn trees
Strain away from the wind and heckled seas.

Yet I come. Here alone I cannot sham.
The place insists that I know who I am.

Elemental trinity – earth, air, sea –
Harshly advocate my humility;

You are bigoted, over ambitious,
You are proud, you salute the meretricious.

Then I have altered this much with the years:
That I need more to admit my errors,

From fear, and a longing not to be blind;
So I am scoured by the unchanging wind,

And rid again of some superfluity
By that force uninterested in me.

And I can go, prepared for the possible;
Dream and bone set out from the confessional.

BRIAN D'ARCY

Trinity

3. The Ballerina
womankind

The trance-ending chord hesitates; and then
recoils into the shadows, where unseen
it leaves within one arc - too cruelly bright -
a fragile form held captive by the light.

A fragile form impaled upon one point,
one curve of perfect grace, one balanced line,
while straining sinews seek to fold and hold,
for beauties sake, the contours of a dream.

And as that final pearl of silence falls
so rapture chills the cadence of her heart.

2. The Matador
mankind

The trance-ending chord hesitates; and then
recoils into the shadows, where unseen
it leaves within one arc - too cruelly bright -
a fragile form held captive by the light.

A fragile form impaled upon one foe,
one curve of perfect grace, one balanced line,
while straining sinews seek to fold and hold,
for glory's sake, the contours of a dream.

And as that final pearl of silence falls
so rapture stills the tremor in his heart.

1. The Saviour

The tranceending chord hesitates; and then
recoils into the shadows, where unseen
it leaves within one arc - too cruelly bright -
a fragile form held captive by the light.

A fragile form impaled upon one cross,
one curve of perfect grace, one balanced line,
while straining sinews seek to fold and hold,
for pity's sake, the contours of a dream.

And as that final pearl of silence falls
salvation's rapture fills that sacred heart.

How Softly Sounds
(Pantoum)

How softly sounds of evening fall
when sunlight slips beyond the rim of earth,
as I, in solitude, recall
life's random interludes of death and birth.

When sunlight slips beyond the rim of earth
chill shadows mark the fading day,
life's random interludes of death and birth
are milestones on my pilgrim's way.

Chill shadows mark the fading day,
so many days now left so far behind
are milestones on my pilgrim's way
recorded in the margins of my mind.

So many days now left so far behind,
too precious and too swiftly past,
recorded in the margins of my mind
their melody I hear at last.

Too precious and too swiftly past,
as I, in solitude, recall
their melody, I hear at last
how softly sounds of evening fall.

Returning Home

The cobbles are still lying here,
and there, within my reach, the wall
of granite blocks I bravely climbed
in youth, so long ago.

Climbed, and hung suspended
to watch the yellowed river flow,
tight within discoloured banks
along this narrow valley's length.

Now it stands waist high
and there, beyond its span, I see the river,
brighter now that industry
has died along its banks.

The cobbles are still lying here,
and there, clinging to the valley sides,
small houses hang in streets unchanged
by recent time or passing loss.

Clinging to their near-forgotten past
with roots that pierce the land
too deep to yield their grasp,
and yet too fragile to survive.

And there, beyond the river walls and streets,
lie upland moors of peat and withered grass;
timeless beyond remembering,
uncaring of the changing scene below.

The cobbles are still lying here -
worn and older now -
I pause, recalling memories hiding
in the silence locked within these stones.

Recalling half-remembered truths,
and half-forgotten dreams;
recalling long-past visions
of things that might have been.

And here, where images
of generations past and future merge
to share their meanings,
the cobbles hold me still.

Gone Like Dreams

In 1849 Charlotte Bronte wrote in a letter to William Smith Williams:
"It is over; Branwell – Emily – Anne are gone like dreams."

It is over. The uncaring sun casts
her shadows on the long enduring moor,
reshaping memories we shared before
I learned, too soon in life, that nothing lasts.
Branwell – Emily – Anne are gone like dreams
unfinished on my partly written page,
while self-anointing grief and aching rage
lay waste my soul with silent inner screams.

Over, but as the chill night falls, I hear,
trapped in the silence of my room, faint sounds,
faint echoes reaching out from yesterday.
And Oh! I fear the moment sleep draws near
when haunting visions from their cold earth mounds
will rise and cry: "Remember me, and pray."

Remembering Anne
(Sojourn on Haworth Moor)

Yes, thou art gone! and never more
will feel the wild wind fresh against your face,
nor see the skylark rise above the moor,
nor treasured childhood memories retrace.

Yes, thou art gone! and never more
will pause, and in that quiet interlude
find respite from the clamour and the roar,
and dream again your dreams in solitude.

Yes, thou art gone! and never more
will race beneath descending winter skies,
nor mourn discarded leaves that summer wore,
nor hear the moorland's melancholic sighs.

Yes, thou art gone! and never more
will wander where bright waters catch the sun,
nor see the beauty that you saw before.
But here your spirit stays - though thou art gone.

Based on the opening line of *A Reminiscence* by Anne Bronte:
Yes, thou art gone! and never more

Recumbent Stones at Arbor Lowe

High on the bleak Derbyshire moors at Arbor Lowe (near Bakewell) within a prehistoric earthenwork over 40 recumbent pieces of limestone lie in a circular pattern. Dated to a time prior to 2000BC their purpose is now long forgotten.

There is an ancient silence here
indifferent to passing years,
enduring, in this barren place,
eternities of solitude.

Here sleeping stones lie overthrown
embedded deep in sculptured earth.
Their patterns hint at glories past
and conjure mysteries for the soul.

Here sleeping stones, once shaped, once drawn,
once raised by human faith, still guard
ancestral promises and dreams
laid deep within this sacred world.

Here sleeping stones hide patient ghosts
whose secrets, lost to memory,
await with pregnant breathlessness
the resurrection of the stones.

JANET FAY

Nightworkers

We're getting up now
we nightworkers
sitting in the kitchen
bent over a cup of tea or a cigarette
listening to the hum of the fridge or the drip of water.
We are alone, our job is pain.
Some of us weep, some clench our teeth.
It's homework, outwork,
lonely, not paid.
Difficult to unionize us.

Travel with us
In the darkness, our journey is fearful.
We know we have got there, when we reach morning.

You do join us sometimes.
Why do you try to forget that?
You'll need those skills again
to enter the dark night you must travel alone
and us the reminders of the journey to come
Night workers and day workers are the same.

MARK FLOYER

English Teacher

Like Hamlet,
He's strutted his stuff before his sleepy class
with words, words, words.
Like Feste,
He's tinkered with linguistic cheveril gloves
with bittersweet wit.

Now into his fifth age,
he hovers in Arcturus Bookshop, Totnes
between the sea and the moors.
browsing through emollient Buddhist texts
seeking sermons in stones
and other matters sage.

So long as he doesn't but slenderly know himself,
like Lear, veer
into senility
and watch his offspring disbranch themselves,
sliver from the sap.
So long as he doesn't go mad
and topple off the bottom shelf.

If only he can stumble on,
like the happy old shepherd in Bohemia,
tumble into things newborn
and keep with the quick of life.

Blues

Blues is my vision of America on the other side of the tracks:
down on the boondocks, hobos hopping freights,
empty smashed bottles of moonshine whisky, mournful
broken eyes staring up from shanty town ruins.
Blues is life stark, rock bottom, no cash, woman lost
and gone, no home, nowhere to go, alcoholic shakes in the gutter.
Blues is a Howl of pain at the shit unfairness of life.
Blues is an American Pageant: black backs bent over
cotton whilst the white landlord sups hot toddies in the

honeysuckle dusk, riverboat Mississippi and Bayou swamps,
Mark Twain, John Brown's body, Chicago 1920, Harlem 1930,
G I s' dazed out on dope in a Saigon whorehouse.

Blues is a soaring guitar solo, a breathtaking tightrope
between joy and sorrow, revelling in its own instinctive
genius.
Blues is dusty record sleeves thumbed through in second
hand dives - the sudden whiff of an exotic sub-culture,
heroes like Howlin'Wolf, Leadbelly, T-Bone Walker,
'Gatemouth' Brown.
Blues is smoke-filled seedy nightspots 4 a.m. - an unholy
blend of sex rhythm n'booze.
Blues is Billie Holiday just about keeping her body
together for one last number.

Blues is a license to loosen that stiff upper lip,
self-indulge in self-pity.
Blues is really a chance to stop thinking, start feeling.
Blues is vicarious identification with the negro sensibility.
Blues is my ego busting out to be all that it isn't-
spontaneous, forthright and unselfconscious.
Blues is all the danger of the street
from behind the safety of my middle-class headphones.

Meccanosolitaire

One Xmas John was gifted a Meccano set
and urged to fashion 'constructs' out of nuts and bolts.
Outside the Compound sweltered, crows croaked -
only his ayah could soothe his fits and starts.

Father was an engineer, built pipelines in Assam.
He would have been around to explain
but couldn't, and "Dammit, it's good for the boy
to show initiative, apply some logic, use his brain..."

Mother had arranged a round of golf
with the pink-gin swilling wallahs at Tolly
so she'd left him with the booklet of instructions,
summoned Driver and embarked on her jolly.

Forty years on, the bits lie unassembled on the floor.
Acute myopia impedes decoding of the small print;
he can't even mend a plug, let alone a woman's heart.
Inside his head the crows croak on, he dreams of ayah's scent.

*Tollygunge Club, Calcutta - a popular watering-hole
used for recreation by the European expat community.*

Edvoucayshun

I teach them the dark ones
the manics, the drunks, the suicides.

Dosed up on Dothiepin I usher
my healthy young charges

through denial and despair -
let a "Plank in Reason" chink

and – "The Belljar" descend,
let them-"hit a world at every plunge":

Lowell
    Sexton
   Lowry
      Plath

I call this 'Edyoucayshun' -

I should lead them out, toward, beyond
but I let them fall so they can rise.

VANESSA FREEDMAN

Broken

Like a broken toy
Red wooden wheels
Discarded in a casual heap
Shattered
Dislocated
Something's not right
Out of place
Put back together wrong
And the child
Howls
Over the broken pieces

Breakthrough

I have prised out one brick
From my prison wall

Through the narrow dusty gap
Sunlight trickles in
Onto the grimy floor

After long silence
I can hear
Cries of children playing
A distant telephone
Footfalls in the street

I have been trapped
Inside my head
In this dark place
And I am relieved to learn
That there is still
A world outside

One day soon
I will escape

ANNI G

Words

You were my slaves
I ordered you, commanded you, fashioned you into my poems
I was your master, controlling your behaviour, demeanour, attitude
And now you have up-risen, revolted, taken me prisoner.
You run amok each night through my head
At three a.m. whole armies of you march the avenues of my mind
Smaller factions take sections prisoner
An occasional sniper shoots his meaning direct to a cell
To remain torturing me over and over until I accede
Wearily turning on the lamp, reaching for pad and pen
To re-capture you, reign you in, re-claim my mind and sleep.

Reading

I have no Latin, no knowledge of the classics
No memory of authors' names
Only an occasional title remains
Locked in my soul forever.
I cannot quote poetic lines
Nor converse with authority on literary matters
But my heart brims over with all that I've read
And my eyes can tell you what my heart's never said.
My body knows the pain of thirst and hunger;
My mind, the prisoner's torment.
I've sung for freedom with my brother
And heard the guns resound like thunder.
My heart has pined for lover and country
And I've longed for hearth and home.
All this within me lives,
Quickening my blood, whilst the memories flood
With all that's been written, all that I've read
And things that sometimes should never be said.

GEOFFREY GODBERT

Therapy

This poem is therapy;
it's doing me good
I cannot connect
without the words.
I can make them write
"romantic dismay"
therapeutically.
There: *romantic dismay*;
and it feels so good

from About not Knowing

This remembering thing: why do
we need it to start let alone
go on forever while I
for one feel better and better
by forgetting what it is
I don't want to remember
such occasions as my childhood
my getting old or in between
as though the anxiety
and the pleasure never happened
as though I had never quite occurred
and so had nothing to regret
and nothing more to hope for
except the unobtainable
of course willing a poem
for the poet who finds stars street lights
and writes poems about
broken-hearted love, describing
the tenderness of its decline.
When I read the words, I think
how could I have missed such kerfuffles,
why didn't I know these lovers'
meeting places or ever
even see them act out the real
life of them, the real love of them,
let alone hear their heart-beats
grow quieter and quieter at the end?

All this was going on all around
me, but I only have these poems'
words for it that that is what I missed
(why, I didn't even know
they were being written down!):
so we can discount poems
which confessionally try to say
what can never really be said
about dying while praying
or in one moment of brilliance
preclude the pointlessness
of having to tell anyone
something they would not understand
even if you had told them
beforehand they would not as also
happens so often in love
on earth but not in heaven;
yet I am envious of this:
that some no longer have need
to write down their dreams by night
now they can see them by day:
purity of awakening
miracles of clarity,
masterpieces portrayed piercingly
through anything bright which comes to hand.

These sheer likenesses are also
unlike anything I have seen before
under the sun or, alas, under
the stars and the mysteries there
I imagined were permanent.
They will accuse me of idealism,
of claiming the tendency
of poetry to lie which
had bothered me until I gave it
up, leaving this: this trying to kiss
anyone fully on the lips
like reminders returning
of the finest walks, when, after
a long time, a man, say, strides out
again arm in arm with a woman;
and finds it as lovely
as a poem used to be.

JIM GREENHALF

Lone Wolf

in memory of Barry MacSweeney, 1948-2000

He was never good at jokes
he took everything too seriously,
too personally,
ever to be good at jokes.

Prudence never got the better
of his peculiar valour.
In writing he preferred pulverising truth;
concealed irony he considered arch,
a slyness inconsistent
with his vision of a writer:

a lone wolf above the treeline.

Though his mind was modulated by bearded Beats,
like Burroughs he subscribed to shaving
as the mark of civilisation.
Coveted good shoes, smart clothes,
the stylish and sensible mode
bred by his native Northumbrian country.
His mind might be a buzz of the latest
from New York, Los Angeles, London,
but his heart remained the red-shanked lad
from Allenheads, hero of Sparty Lea,
the rude boy of Alston, Nenthead,
Haydon Bridge, Haltwhistle,
hare-lipped Pearl's constant friend.
And to me he introduced Pascal Roge
playing Poulenc and Erik Satie.
The music of Miles Davis,
Mose Allison, Leadbelly,
Charlie Mingus, Arizona Dranes,
Sister O.M. Terrell, Memphis Minnie,
Robert Johnson, Lonnie Johnson,
Blind Willie Johnson,
Bob Dylan, he emphatically declared

the greatest artist of the century.
Prudence never got the better
of his tongue. Son House,
Gil Evans and Jimmy Guiffre.

Up late, popping fresh bottles,
a disc revolving the stereo,
fingers poised above the keys:
a fighter pilot
about to blast
another crooked untruth
from the sky of reason.

Vituperative in the viper's tongue.
Alternately exultant and mortified
by his delight in wounding;
but vulnerable to counter-strikes.
The prickly leaf hid a tender flower.
When words failed
he would resort to other means.
Empties in his house
like a dead emperor's
terracotta warriors.

Unlike me, he could identify and name
bird, beast and flower.
Lesser beings, in his proudful eyes,
dared to judge his shortcomings.
Beware, he warned, of Replicants!

There are 1,998 cigarette paper-thin pages
in the 1996 Norton Anthology:
355 entries, from Caedmon's Hymn
to Cynthia Zarin, plus the usual soft drizzle
of Raine, Ashbery, Longley and Dunn.
In place of Bukowski Brad Leithauser,
Gjertrud Schnackenberg in place of MacSweeney-
Opening of her lids was like the rising of larks
in the blue slowness of a stubble-burning day.
Pearl's before swine, lamented Finnbar.
Absence from anthologies
confirmed his self-flagellating view:

112

he was the Lollard, the persecuted
Leveller, the lone wolf outlaw
Revelling in his under-the-counter
culture status with a touch too much bravado
concealed his rage against injustice;
contempt congealed his hurt.

Does his soothing mint still grow;
in the garden now unattended
are the chives and other aromatic herbs
speared by Northern rain
that was his obligato?
He died alone in his house,
beyond the law, the treeline.
I told him once: Barry
the lone wolf is a mistaken image.
Wolves by nature are communal:
the lone wolf has no future.

MICHAEL HASLAM

Spriggan Fair

1.

Up to a shriek and yielding, the excess gave let
to bleating at the throat. The field was rank.
You knew it needed to be mowed. I had a spriggan
threatening to run amok. I'm not conceding
what was owed. Expressly it was being booked
for being bloody cropped. It shot that shout
so loud that the machinery had stopped.

Expanding crowns up to a loaf of steam
and bottoms out. A spell explodes in bleeps
and bits of soundless broken flak. I had been
suffering exacerbated bitterness, remanufacturing
my fractured wing, the gripping throttle,
you'll excuse me as I crack the bottle, but the pain
came as I saw them waddle out across the lea
with all their fine mud-flinging tackle, spreading
what-is-it, the freight of their fertility
until they're spent up on the thwaites…
I count to three

the cloud is held up on the pass.
The cost of reaping drops.
Watercourses shine

Again with cattle on the aftermath lets say
I heard a song about a snake who ate an apple
On a bale of hay. Okay I take it I can happen
Wait for what'll ripen in the latter days with
Ruddy globes of wicken and the sanguine may.

2.

A sleeper's leaping double takes
a folk-shape of the spirit
outing to the fields of fair reality.

All readily an early gaggle clamp
and couple scaffolding to raise a catafalque
and plank for the performers.

Tonal blenders to the tonic test
and practice feeling pitches. Other men
are stringing canvas bloats
into a steady ripple, airing hopes
for the acoustics and a mellow day.

There's a double with standing
in strands of gourds and trinkets
when a rosebush of a sudden gust has let
her petals flood across the flags.

Later on there's a misunderstanding
as trouble is raised in among the people
to be reaped and cut and dropped
for Ancient Dobbin to clop off with in a box.

Abated at a tap in washing up
I had felt for my partner being taken
in feeling, joshed and doffed.
I say I love.
I don't scorn to josh the dolly
while the boggart's cleared off.

3.

The bush cropped at the neck. The pouch back-pocketed.
Hold on the grip while sobbing ebbs
and then it's easy just you rob the dead.
It eases as you had it off, with one more squeeze
the lid was flipped, the tufted duck took flight,
the laughing stopped and stiff and white
the corpse had rattled off an audit of
remaining numbness as another crossed
the pass in smoke between the strands
of ghostly ash. The toff had spoken
with an aspen trepidation: You have caught me
in a sense in some perplexity for cash.
This is my holiday. Let long debts pass.

You kept a bottle up your skirt and hit him
such a smash as hurt and left him landed
in a lake of liquid spirit, bits of rock
and broken glass.

Folk are mocking his deceased demand
for better service in the courting of his class,
the sporting ring, the country interest at last.
One clash. Dead fright. Too loud. All over.

Vibration can't reflect nor shine increase it
in its passage out in shape in pandemonics
touching once upon the time to come
and there's his knocking from inside the coffin.

4.

We're in the book, a double bill
to top at The Pavilion. When
the rubber men have scratched, outstretched,
squealed off to pop,
and all the mummers' props despatched,
    we're on.

Tugged by a fan of strings, a hand
    delivers them, a bunch of kids, of
spriggan lighter-than-air imps. Another man
or just another hand digs in a waist-pouch,
fetching up the change. Eyes speak assent,
a crescent brow. Let go
    in one long derepressant hiss,
I'm missing you.
    The big one from the crown dividing
into filaments of inexplicable division,
multiplicities of never-fine-enough
to fill a pinhole.

So decided we must say no blether but to say
together that The Spirit Decided in the rout in twine:
The one to shadow blight of loathing foiled,
    the other grew revolting in advance and shrank
fastidious into a nicer neat recoil. So though

     we came to scorn enjoyment of
enjoined performance, this was not before
we claimed the making of a new thesaurus:
     I speak of a fervent performance, and
a certain spirit form.

     What did you spend such time in
Celtic Folklore and the Fairies for?
     Called Spriggan Fair.

Vacations 1. iii

It soothes me to be let to come to her
Combing her hair out in a public cobbled yard
The eye caught in a glass
A Friday Morning
Something spat and snapped
and particles of parting kiss run back.

I took to being given broken windows
for the smashing glass effects.
The smack shaped like a leaf of holly.
I had been attacked.

The globe being opened, and the globing closed.
You have an hour to clear the square.
The service was concluded with the rites of silence.
Conscience of The Heart.
The host was not to be consumed.

Had there been a naked body
centering the smash and grab, I had been
scaling down a ladder to the basin.

Still I'm self-accused of being
over-liberal with dribble:
Drivel! Trinket-baubler!
Calls the Crow.
I'm turning and I'm talking to you.
It is true.

Vacations 1. iv.

It's true that of the two I do prefer
the softer gurgle of the hollow bright phenomena,
the purling, the descending song of willow-warbler to
the brittle red and metal raucous calling,
and an ease of spirit on the river to
a tale of bloody murder. In another
watershed I cannot contribute to you.

My namesake saint though is Celestial Accipiter
and an ideal of scales.
The sword has pierced my heart in its
felicity at heights.

My spiritual love is for the Siren *Phoca*
who has drawn precipitated swimmers under water.
I can see them flutter from the net in smattered lather
and wet bits of light.
My company are tumblers crumbled
to a crucible. My principles
are set to scrape a cloistered mausoleum
or a hollow tomb, a catacomb,
a womb, a womb, a womb;
an enterprising spirit in an engine-room,
I hold my own ideas of form.

Supposing we admit each other to another
Masonry, The Square and True
of the Old Geometric School. How do you feel?
How do you do? Fear nothing.
It's imaginary. Now return to the Untrue.

Vacations 1. v.

But as you see I let my margins of disorder grow.
What brought me to
the snap and crackle of a podding broom?
I had to laugh at thinking of me having been
out in the garden, watering the moon.

With tumbling feeling I have grabbed
at rosebay down. The coming winter,
can I stay within the safe-side, self-control?

The day is grand.
The Yorkshire Air is like a sea of dark blue cloth
drawn off the certain grounds on which I see
my self-renewal. Pay attention
to the flinches nestling in the rarer blush,
like a hope for qualities of social interaction
and I'll get along.

I'd like to try my best to entertain you with
a deficit pitched in the dish
a deafness in the ditch
a wind-boom through a blow-hole in the cliff
but I presume
we should be equable
you entertain me too
and we can let our sensing rest
and hollowness resume.

(It's glib I know but that's just what
I got out in the garden with the podding broom.)

Schooling

1.

The bristle warns of The Invisible. The buzzing swarms
coil out through an embrasure. Rising from
a whistle to the boil, the whole bowl of the bell
is thrown upon the storm. The Thistle, Rose and Fern,
The Forms of Thorn, I wrote while I had written
through the school emitting fervent scrolls of plume
until The Forks had grabbed me, sagging at the knees.

      Beset by bees, I brought a tray of cups
one fraught and fractious morning, rattled out of doors
with flying saucers coming at me from The Hall.
I ran up to the railing where
I can't recall

A cold silver spoon at the back of my neck
I would give my all for
I had stumbled when I found her cold
> How Old Are You
> *This bell is for your Close*

Weak fingers touching on the noose. The Carrion
around The Crown. The Crown of Stars, burst through
a heart's bestartlement, and carried on a bustle
through a crowded frequence, turning blue
the infant faints in the regard profound.
Unkindly Spirits of the waste-ground ring
      to watch one drown.

I just bobbed up with this bill for duck and I'm off
back down. My curls are frizzling now
on yonder brazier. I got but bruised afflight
With Azure Wings. I got an oar full on the ear,
lumps on the crown and in the throat, and burns
down there, it's one mad merry-go-round,
they only let me out on good behaviour.

2

A suicide, before she viewed me bleakly
as a shading to the prospect of her dark success,
took me aside to show me these, her steps,
her rope, her trap. She thought we
might be sharing these, but I was horrified,
her shawl was ripped, I wished for something,
I was holding on. My bits. All subtlety
was let upon the flood and soon she died.

They were like these the slides she showed
one of me coldly stealing from the pool.
The stole was in the net and dripping wet.
I let it lapse to orb and globe. I'm close
to sense as glister quells out on an even ebb
to go like petals blown into the meant immense.

But use some gumption. Goodness Knows
the winter snows are almost burying the heather.

You are in some foul distemper since you swore
you never ever drew a single sliver
       off the figure of her dancing
in the silence of the mirror. All her corpse
was drawn up on the banks of one great
       living river, limp and damp
and enveloped in slime. But let her go
protesting, aquatic as ever, down river, flown,
how like a duck is nothing now it's grown.
I run a tub, sink into it unbending knees
in mottled light I steep, however long
and watch the steam until I pull the plug, unknot
my subtle gut and briefly nod through this
my own oblation to the drain.

Green Withen Aura

(Delightful Pastime Oral Call Response.
For Peter Riley)

I had been following, or so I felt, a futile so-called
calling, and a false trail, and I had failed.
Footloose I lay, and heard another sweet cascade
of little falls, and something solitary, smaller:
the green withens aura.
There's an air to the wild upland willows.
    Halo To The Sallows. Hello There
young green yellow willow warbler
footles through light leafs
an odd fluff-suited, coloured, call. Subtle
the way it's fluted this June.
    An air of blue
veils the face of the day-time moon.
The young out of a bog-edge nest are flown.
    An air you feel
is like benevolence, if you could only cage it
like a lark in pastoral romance.
    A waving air;
a one-year wand of one fond fairy
    salix-frond, forms out of somnolence
in woodland dress.

And, in co-incidence, another air, another day
   on folly field I almost heard
the butterfly marine band play
   with the shine blown away
with the fairies in the shale.

Two Poems from the Music Laid Her Songs in Language

I hear she mews through mistal walls.
Telephone calls.
A cluster.
Notes on drama, dream and trauma.

A note of all souls. Who heard hullet cote owls
   where dark and stoney lanes meet in a fork.
What got my throat was a summer note about the cat-
with-a-swallow-in-her-teeth duet.
      One awful time we used to hear
the calving screams of Belgian Blues, night after night
bray from the brand-new laithe at stoney royd.
   A Note.
I have these sirens muffled inwardly.
Old News.
I much prefer the stretch to hearing
   of a far-off river.
I am less annoyed. A note:
Find out about the phantom sibling, how it found
the space inside a self-reflexive soul.
Unfortunately
it was found uncomfortably snuffled.
Me,
I see my lights are on but I am not at home.

We are up some siding from
   the tracks of music laid her language songs.
A sketch. Describe
the boiler-slag and other cinder tippings
as a bank of levelled heaps:
   a gabled valley-crest
of back-to-backs. Make it look
quite picturesque. A new romantic vista
of the valley death. And not

untruthful. Dirty
pastel mist of idle waste
in some confusion mixed with astley brook
and run on down to coke choked breath.
I have the art to use how light dark echoes
    with the still sound shadows
and a local calling
Have you seen our smutty beauty hereabouts?

Over the footbridge down at waters meetings.
Loud colliding. Classinesses in the cinder. Ruby
in the light reflex. The lines in some perspective find
the water-treatment works.

I have willed you here to lull you lob.
You are only playing with words.
You know what rhymes with them.
Emerging empty as lugubrious more mournful
in the gravel where the plot was laid you lost
your marbles in the middle of that slaggy puddle.
You can see what rhymes with dream and drama
written in reflections of the sky above
your armature in love.

The More Terrible Slips

I lie inside without control of my
wide-rolling eyes - I've seen me go
so clouded I obscured the skies.
But when this grace alights upon my face
I cry Goodbye to my Complicity, Goodbye
also Surprise: The Sword descends
to interrupt us, shredding instincts
into slivers in the grass. Am I
not satisfied? Time flies, the evening flocks.
It looks so late.

    *A shriven forfeit as a rule may be
accepted if it's naked and alive.*
    That could be my certificate and I'm
to have it framed before Her Grace and heard
in audience before the echo dies. Her Grace

is like the bitter taste of blankness in the eyes,
and I'm shown up as shaken but no wiser
for my faking lies. Let Slip....

The day she spiralled in the midges
        as a swallow dives across the clouded surface
set against: Let Slip The Knot, a craven nuisance
tries, trussed to a tree, to die; *subsumed -with*
flaring in the cry and so accepted or rejected
as recurrence/no recurrence to the lips of fate
sets up together such a sort of dialectic as
the sexual spirit and a sleight of mind.

The Lucent School

The blush reversed, the blood was drained, a gulp at first
had helped me blank out what I'd done, and blank again
at why I'd come to school in tears without the terms
I had deliberately rehearsed.

*By the claw in the back of my neck I was seized
and fetched. I come to have this pressure eased, the claw
removed, the poison drawn, and for the blessing
to be drenched in one aspersion of the horn.*

With a goose, with a rush and a wild return
a fluency came fooling through the water-hole.
The shallow glitters sounds and shoals. A wispish soul
inclines to slip into the pool. Stripped to its lips
it calls a school of waving males and females,
ululating all its cry's display. *It's willing.*

The pool was fully solipsism, but so full
of others some of whom were sporting far
more nakedly than I who shades his eyes
to find in some particulars
        of ocular response *a love all over.*
With the splash of an unqualified explosion
and a shrilling larynx
        I had waded in.

from **A Century**

54.

Expiate the snake out of the chest,
the unforgiven genius of race,
the coffee-cups and egg-stained plates,
the demon of frustrated lethargy about the place -
    Come hooked and landed as a wriggling fury,
mucous feathers drawn out of the mouth,
    the crying outcome of a random rush -
What sex is it? Its fists
    clutch empty air.

Each throb a ring echo of human ecstasy or pain,
astonished in the flood to love
    for crying out loud
above a thorough-going drone, the spasms flatten
and ellipse into the distance
    as a higher ring, the dream of stone,
the waste of generation, spoiled over the world.

Is it dragons, love, or is it doves?
    The couple separate and fuse
    the other side of sleep with darkness
sinking water down the scale a rung or tone
or two. The organ needed to be sacrificed -
    Its tail had grown so long!
    Now there's a lake-child playing safely
    at the gates of sleep. A flush
    of cheeks, and thanks {*afanc* - a water-dragon)
    thanks for the advance, and thanks again.
The place is safe. The inn is filling with
tall tourist stories of arrival.

55.

Despair, reconciled to Life through Beauty,
Wild Rose, I plucked from Councillor Miss Thorne's
    Garden, one Quarter Day, before the dawn:
        An August Gift,
a mist-born being combed and drawn

and funnelled through into oblivion,
                   who missed being born

and passed from shadow into emptiness,
redemption, in a glance
and didn't stall.

        The Progress of The Soul
            A shape
       and I'm made whole

           wild Winged Life

which must transmute to a possession the
remembrance of its passage through the world
or else
it's Elongated Faces haunting All Along
a life long journey.

Better do to witness Truth: by bebop butterfly to
Fullness through a Fullness soul -
       or as the blind from birth recall
their own pre-natal colours, that is,
soul whose all is metaphorical,
       or not at all.

The Green Woodpecker

introduction

The Cuckoo-Thunder broke on Spring Bank Brink
and scattered urinaceous droppings of a sudden
coming green. The zephyr
caught into a meteoric shape
here culminates, brings these, and leaves
a spectral vivid trail
of amber glass and greenish vitrine.

I suppose these are what the poets call
the harbingers or heralds, now the scene is set
for the reintroduction of a shy fair sun
with mist-cum-shine, through mellow glass
to finding something in the water.

I think it sunk within my thoughtstream,
something seen, come blurring in the flow.

I've been up on the brink again this spring,
and I write while the crockery
piles too high in the sink.

I have the use of a garden delph.
        It was here I decided to sow the seed
of my this life's ghost of discontent.
        I think you have to do this in deep dream.

The deepest of these dreams I know so far
is this: I felt a feathering
within the air around me, and I turned and said,
Aquila, is that you?
It was a figure in the chronicles of this
        Return to Poetry, beginning when
a willow branch had scraped the roof
of a green-painted aluminium stranded caravan.
        There I am writing, thick
in the instant heat of bottled gas.
        It's late at night. I stop and doff
my shoes and trousers, feeling soft
and pent in comfortable underpants.

What next I saw was a figure for
the number of four globes
encincturing an orifice,
pavilioned with feathery hands
in a receding-in-perspective hall
that disappeared into a sky
with minute bouts of turbulence for clouds.

I think it then was evening, though my doubts accrue,
my doubts had somehow calmed me through.
I looked ahead and smiled and said,
Alanna, is that you?

Is that not daft enough? Then look at this.
There was a corpse laid flat
on the fork lift truck of these beseeching hands,
and only just this side of the fence of final silence
and I want to know
how long is this floating in eternity for?

Then she came up the road from pure vacation
bearing sheaves of news of our own local
apocatastrophe, as though we might
with glue restore the star-tree's greening lights.
But there was no thematic miracle
but one long marital disaster.
She had finished physical
In forays climaxing in incandescent rage, and I
had fallen between stools on the floor.

Then a long-delayed shock as her glance deteriorates
1 think it's sinking, and I think
The Comic made A Mess of Things
with Good Intentions, standing soaked
in a fleet of like flooding sands
in socks and just these underpants.

Then I took the rough track into a badly-overhung glade,
that gave the shadow canopy. I went by bluebells to
the river hole. And if I saw myself I'd wonder
what on earth I had in mind, A Ghost.

It was like the mood of a croaking daw
and a length of rope, in darkness
m the very early morning.
You can see the hanged man's landing
in a loud wind along a very foul shore.

It was also since I'd got
some buttered shock electric news
from the post and dropped
the marmalade across the toast
and spluttered choking at the cost.

On a walk I have come in the dusk
like a bus to a terminus. Shaking my motor,
and shivering, on with the lights.

Here you can smell the effluvial stream
from the mill, while the nightshift sweats
        over cotton. The dusk falls through
        the cliff of woods
        to the fluminous swirling bend;
like a line sent on an errand
it will come back empty-handed in the rain.

It could have been just here
that the light first stabbed the heart,
and kept on stabbing
while the stream fell deeper into trees,
and reached the bridge by the railway line,
as though wanting to scream.

ANTHONY HECHT

The Vow

In the third month, a sudden flow of blood.
The mirth of tabrets ceaseth, and the joy
Also of the harp. The frail image of God
Lay spilled and formless. Neither girl nor boy,
But yet blood of my blood, nearly my child.
      All that long day
Her pale face turned to the window's mild
      Featureless grey.

And for some nights she whimpered as she dreamed
The dead thing spoke, saying: "Do not recall
Pleasure at my conception. I am redeemed
From pain and sorrow. Mourn rather for all
Who breathlessly issue from the bone gates,
      The gates of horn,
For truly it is best of all the fates
      Not to be born.

"Mother, a child lay gasping for bare breath
On Christmas Eve when Santa Claus had set
Death in the stocking, and the lights of death
Flamed in the tree. O, if you can, forget
You were the child, turn to my father's lips
      Against the time
When his cold hand puts forth its fingertips
      Of jointed lime."

Doctors of Science, what is man that he
Should hope to come to a good end? *The best
Is not to have been born.* And could it be
That Jewish diligence and Irish jest
The consent of flesh and a midwinter storm
      Had reconciled,
Was yet too bold a mixture to inform
      A simple child?

Even as gold is tried, Gentile and Jew.

If that ghost was a girl's, I swear to it:
Your mother shall be far more blessed than you.
And if a boy's, I swear: The flames are lit
That shall refine us; they shall not destroy
        A living hair.
Your younger brothers shall confirm in joy
        This that I swear.

The Origin of Centaurs

"But to the girdle do the gods inherit,
Beneath is the entire fiend's."
        King Lear

This mild September mist recalls the soul
        To its own lust;
On the enchanted lawn
It sees the iron top of the flagpole
        Sublimed away and gone
Into Parnassian regions beyond rust;
And would undo the body to less than dust.

Sundial and juniper have been dispelled
        Into thin air.
    The pale ghost of a leaf
Haunts those uncanny softnesses that filled
        And whitely brought to grief
The trees that only yesterday were there.
The soul recoils into its old despair,

Knowing that though the horizon is at hand,
        Twelve paltry feet
    Refuse to be traversed,
And form themselves before wherever you stand
        As if you were accursed;
While stones drift from the field, and the arbor-seat
Floats toward some *millefleurs* world of summer heat.

Yet from the void where the azalea bush
        Departed hence,
    Sadly the soul must hear

Twitter and cricket where should be all hush,
        And from the belvedere
A muffled grunt survives in evidence
That love must sweat under the weight of sense.

Or so once thought a man in a Greek mist -
Who set aside
            The wine-cup and the wine,
And that deep fissure he alone had kissed,
All circumscribing line,
Moved to the very edge in one swift stride
And took those shawls of nothing for his bride.

Was it the Goddess herself? Some dense embrace
           Closed like a bath
        Of love about his head;
Perfectly silent and without a face.
           Blindfolded on her bed,
He could see nothing but the aftermath:
Those powerful, clear hoof prints on the path.

JOHN HIRST

Wilfred on War

(In remembrance of the poet and soldier Wilfred Owen)

Stenches in trenches
Rifles with bayonets, just...
One hundred metres apart.

Not 'mile-high' bombs
Death from a distance
I'm told there very smart.

Friendly fire!!, mass funeral pyre
All automated with a 'silicon-chip smile'
Clean kill, no uniform dirt, mud or mire.

War poet in residence, paid to write
Lap-top, spell check, politically correct
Creative licence, not a foot soldier in sight.

As I look down on you and your B52's
I ask who, why, and what... was the choice?
No lessons learned then... from 'my ghostly voice'.

(written during the first day's of the second Iraq War)

MICHAEL HOLMES

All Days Have Endings
August 1962

All days have endings,
when the proud air drops tired, into the darkness,
and the song of the last bird dies with it.
All days have their endings,
when the green moss spreads itself quietly in a fading light
and the walls are grey:
when the houses, covered by haze, locked one with another,
stretch and fall away
with their gates and windows closed,

And the last sound of the voice that is supposed never to die away,
Comes back once more,
echoes bravely with a sound which, fighting away the final pulse,
lies broken here.
O they have their endings
these days,
and I too.
These days which stretch out beyond our windows
and close as we close,
taking their end without fuss or formality,
and showing one face to the world.
Their moment is gone, as in summer their time is imagined
before it has begun
and lies within the space of a twilight.

The tree which stands, is gone;
the lights which shine, are out;
the grey darkness rests upon all.

It is not for a year or a moment;
not for a month when the blind see and the deaf hear,
not for a time when eyes are closed in sleep,
but for their endings, they exist
and end as they begin.

Will you wait for a moment?
Will you stay for just one moment'?

No, it is not worth your while;
there is a morning to come and a day which replaces what is gone,
so it is not worth your while.

Look! the lights are out and the trees are gone.
There is no last face to it all.
O they have their endings, these days
And I too.

To Barbara (& the Beatles)

Do not wear red tonight
for red is the colour of the dying sun
as it falls away from life into the unending dark;
do not wear my sun now it has gone.

Do not wear green tonight,
for green is the heavy colour of lost hopes
and vain desire - do not dress yourself
in leaves fallen through these fingers.
Do not wear blue tonight,
for blue hangs like a cradle from
an empty sky, the focus of an
innocent, unerring, indiscriminating eye.

Do not wear grey for these
are my feelings, do not
wear black, for this is the
dark river of despair; do not wrap
yourself in rainbows snatched from tormented skies.

Come to me alone and weeping;
Come to me naked and with fear,
and with transparent fingers
we will fly the crippled fig-leaf like a kite
through smashed illusion and a hopeless year.

JOHN HORDER

The Sick Image of My Father Fades

The sick image of my father fades.
When I was three he used to take me
Tied up in a sack to the cliff's edge
And threaten to throw me over. The wind
Was ghastly, and his hands shook with terror.
I whimpered like a fretful dog. Fear
Stole over me, and I shrieked and screamed.

My father said, shall I break your legs
Before throwing you over? You should then land
On the sand without the sudden crunch crunch
Of breaking bones. I looked up at him, pleading.
Then he would laugh out loud like a normal man,
And let me clamber back on to his back, so that I forgot
The sheer drop from the cliff's edge, just for a moment.

Included in The Rag and Bone Shop of the Heart (ed. Robert Bly, James Hillman and Michael Mead. Harper Collins New York 1992), The Treasury of English Poetry (ed. Caldwell and Kendrick. Doubleday NY 1984), Beyond Bedlam (ed. Ken Smith and Matthew Sweeney. Anvil 1998)

Don't Postpone Amazing Yourself for One Single Moment in Warm Memory of Nicholas Albery

When we die
More than at any other moment
We need our hugging friends
To come out of their closets
And assert just how amazing we all are.
That word "all" includes our billions of ancestors.

Nicholas Albery had continuously
Chosen to amaze himself
During his lifetime as Nicholas.
He knew the process of self-amazement
Couldn't be postponed for one single moment.
He did not procrastinate:

"1) Write down your 20 main pleasures in life. Then
2) Write down ten ways to make money from your pleasures
(Ideally from a combination of your pleasures).
3) Explore one of these ways, trying it out, if yon can,
In reality." The process of Nicholas's self-amazement is continuous.
Like love, it is highly infectious. Once the barriers start disintegrating one by one
They cease for all time. Don't postpone amazing yourself for one single moment.

John Horder read this poem at Nicholas's memorial service at St. James's Church, Piccadilly in 2002.

The Measure of Their Fear

Hanging under those long, long moments
When I'm quite sure I'm going to die,
Or pass out at any moment, or He for ever
In a tiny wrinkled box, alone,
While the rain silently rots away at the wood,
I wonder at the owls, romantic and melancholy,
Locked up in their private myth, desperate as poets
In their inability to communicate,
Taking up uneasy posts in the dark,
Wings tremulous, yet who would know it,
Knowing the measure of their fear, yet quite mastering it.

My Muse Last Night

My muse visited me last night.
Left a terrible trail of blood
On the tips of the spiked railings
Outside my house.
Really, you'd think she'd be more considerate.
Made a most filthy mess for all the neighbours to see.

A Sense of Being

There is nothing in me to assure me of my being.
That is why I so often think
About my heart beating.
Nothing to do with the fear of it stopping.

It's just it's so hard to imagine it - beating-
Just as it's hard to imagine that I derive from something
That actually works. Something that lives and breathes.
Something that has a sense of its own being.
Oh, it's so very hard to imagine these things,
And I've always been told that I was imaginative by nature.

Imagine: a tree has roots: it knows where it springs from.
We have parents. But the orphan and the murderer have one
   thing in common.
Something vital in each of them has been wiped out.
It's hard to explain exactly what. It's something
A word or a glance from a parent may have set into motion
Or not. It's not that this gives a child a sense of itself
Just like that. Nothing as simple as that.
But it can be the basis. Something to start from, something
   that grows
And will eventually determine who and what he's to be
Or not to be, as the case may be. Whether he is, or is not.

The Child Walks around Its Own Grave

The child walks around its own grave
He's surprised to see his own body
Laid out, several feet, below ground level.
One of its hands begins to spread out of fear's grip.

He's afraid. Strange that any life should have been left
At all, after so long. That whole body had grown numb
For so long, that the pain, when first felt,
Had been almost more than he (or it) could bear.

To rest in death can be protective.
He'd sheltered in his own dead body
For over eighteen years. The child's cries, in that time,
Had hardly been heard. Now he's overwhelmed by the noise.

In a Time When I was Nothing

In a time when I was nothing
I was strangely surprised to see
My name in The Times Literary Supplement.

In a time when I was nothing
There was an emptiness both inside and outside of me
And I felt no thing substantially.

In a time when I was nothing
It was most difficult to separate past from present
And the present moment held no sway.

In a time when I was nothing
There seemed no end to this state of non-being
The bottom had been kicked away from everything.

After a long time being nothing
There came at long last a dim realisation
That one day I might eventually become something.
In the time when I was no one
There was simply nothing left to give anyone
And I found myself cut off from everyone.

In the time when I was no one
I knew no man, no woman
And that was when my sense of self began.

Love Poem

I put a heavy burden on my love for you
With all my suffering I do not think I'll see it through
You know, I think, I'm terrified of love as of you.

You challenge all that I am, my love for you.
Part of me, the worst part, does not want to see it through
Right now, I'm torn apart by thought of losing you.

I cannot help myself; cannot help loving you
The eternal part's blocked up in both me and you
Repressed - this is what makes your and my pain ring true.

You see, eternal beauty, once caught sight of, must come through.
1 am as scared of it as I am of you.
Unless we give our selves to it, we'll not come through.

Why Do They Never Cry?

Why do they never cry?
Why do they never weep?
These middle-aged men and women
For ever holding themselves back
A lifetime's resentment, contained
In every moment they breathe.

They will pay the price
For never breaking down, ever.
The coronary will suddenly strike
From nowhere. Taking them to a place
Where weeping is not only the order of the day
But where their hard hearts will still have to be broken down.

Why do they never cry?
Why do they never weep?
Could it be that they are afraid
Of betraying an imaginary weakness?
Couldn't it be that love
Has not melted down a single one of their barriers yet

That separate them not only from themselves but from all others
So they preserve the hard front
To the bitter end.
It's their only way out. - The coronary
When it does its merciful and cleansing work
Certainly leaves them no time to look back

To the forty years or so in which they have held themselves back
From exhibiting one single human emotion, ever.

They were pillars of stone
The moment they were born.

Why do they never cry?

Why do they never weep?
Still constantly keep asking myself
Refusing even now to acknowledge the existence

Of Lot's wife inside of myself.
And she certainly did look back.
She was a pillar of stone
The moment I was born.
She had no need of looking back, even.
She was there, stuck in her tracks

The Moment I was conceived.
Really she need hardly have bothered.
Similarly, the worst has already happened with most of us.
Psychotics, most of us, before we were born even.
It's a thought worth remembering once in a while
However disquieting
Lumps of granite are where most human hearts should be
And this is what is called being born into the twentieth century
Until love started (once more) making its uneasy way
Among the hearts of men.
For so long have we been sub-human
That the first shock (of love's impact) is very nearly overcoming
    every one

as we learn, once more, what it is like to be human
The scorn
Has first to wither within
Each and every one
The scorn
In which we were, each one, first born.

World © John Horder

SIMON P. JONES

Our Neil

He broke his heart, our old friend Neil T.
He upset his soul's applecart, when he professed to be free,
Listening to the Stones or the Doors,
Was just his cup of Ylang Ylang tea,
Smoking a reefer at three in the morning,
His early breakfast to start the day,
Our dear friend Neil T.

Even the night staff passed it round
And they quietly joked about all the good shit he smoked,
What's the price we pay for love?
What's the bloody point if all our families
Have either gone crazy or gone missing or gone up there?
Floating around in silent oblivion.

PAT JOURDAN

Survivors

We are the friends of Icarus,
who fell off-centre
beyond the painting's edge;
no poet saved us.

We gulped and struggled in dirty seas-
no-one noticed; the ships sailed on.
Seaweed-strewn we straggled to the shore.
No-one arrived. We stank.
At city's edge we took new names,
ones they'd understand, hid
the visions, hallucinations and tests,
weeks dashing to and fro the camel's eye.
We know what happens off-scene,
the shabby survival,
cards with a marked corner
and in our rented rooms
we keep new wings, freshly laundered,
sequin-bright, stacked, waiting.

JEANETTE JU - PIERRE

Ghost House

The heavy breathing of a six fingered beast
on the rickety stairs,
clouds of thick dust and cobwebs,
everywhere,
somebody speaking louder than
a rusty drum,
the human hum of a heart beat,
crazy against your eardrums,
first that slow thump
then a rhythmic swing interrupting
your natural breathing pattern,
the madness of the war siren,
alerting lost ghosts to appear from past lives,
a pair of humble eyes looking down at your spine,
observing your chakras,
a giant spider innocently dangles on the banister,
it may crawl in your hair and nest,
a disembodied soul breathing icicles down your chest
walking on fat beach sponges,
conscious of the fear of falling into another dimension
where nobody returns,
something wet and slippery,
hitting your face, neck and legs with
a vengeance,
what unspeakable creature is lurking in
your personal space?

this house of horror has too many secrets
to unravel,
electric blue flares travel before your eyes,
those memories of unicorns racing across a purple sky and
the wolf howling outside the window
is coming to get you.

JAMES KIRKUP

Homage to Ronald Firbank

Black ghost with the bright red hair and henna-tinted nails,
Dear master, you who adored your mother, haunting my perpetual
Hard playground with what should have been
A real memory, why did you die when I was still a child,
And long before I knew you ever lived?

And yet I must have known you were the one
Person I could ever talk to, the secret spirit in the grey
Unpopular corners of that enormous yard.
There, like a weary prince with torn but tearless face
I would weave garlands for my jewelled hands to toss.
With smile extending, to an adoring populace.
The brown-tiled corridors of school, the green-distempered halls
Became a palace in some minor capital
Removed from wars and want, where like a pale
Ecstatic ballet the entire court would swoon
At rumours of a strange and hopeless passion,
Or in the blue-domed miniature cathedral-mosque
Whisper cliches of unusual and ordinary charm.

O, I was Mabel buried half alive, impatiently, near York,
Or Mr. Harvester, composing the unutterable, somehow,
On a Bosendorfer in an attic down in Farm Street;
Or that Miss Compostella, brilliantly upsetting
Everybody's nerves with renderings of Rosmersholm
At a deserted matinée, one tropical midsummer afternoon, at Slough.
I was the queen caught with her crown on, in the dust
Beside her Daimler, changing a yellow-spoked wheel,
Or that wild biographer emotional m Greece,
Or Mrs. Arbanel who shot a lady in a boat near Athens.

Such tears, toilettes, such scenes, such *amours d'alcove*!
And at the Embassy, in August, one otiose noon,
The London Illustrated News and all the paraphernalia of love...

Across the perfectly pirate seas, to Switzerland
Whose disappointing mountains bored La Zoubaroff,
And on to some impossible Olympia of love

You flew and took me with you till the day
You died, leaving the watering-can, the final flowers in a room
In Italy, alone and lost— A kind of saint, you made
Your peace at last with life, became the object of pilgrimage
Which I may never make, except in dreams, and in my heart's homage.

Campo Verano, Rome

The Parting

In a pale dress across the naked lawns
You move, and opening the long windows
Enter the dark house without a word.
In restless shrubbery the statues lean
And look towards you with their hungry eyes
Fixed understandingly upon infinity.

I wait a while among the flowers
That are hushed and watch me with the weight
Of summer heavy still upon their faces.
Children wander up the pathways from the beaches.

The lights go on, casting their nets across the lawn.
In a bright box you move, your hair is golden-brown.
Above a chimney-pot the first star like a spark is blown.

Now 1 will go along the cliffs and by the silent farm,
Across the fields already cold. But turn
To look towards you, often, till the blinds are drawn.

Fading Grass

The sun's candour and the sky's deep light,
The river that by day
Is shallow, and profound at night
Give me no comfort, for all sight
Is empty, now you are away.

Time only makes me feel how life must go
In nothingness without
The time you give me for the love I owe:
How longing lasts beyond the griefs we know,

How all things die, and suns go out.

Always I feel each moment pass
That brings the end of breath.
Our figures part as in a glass
That cannot hold the fading grass
Of love, of pain, of time, of death.

Waiting

I wait with a pencil in my hand
Beside the morning's empty page
Not hoping for a sign, but waiting
For a word that will engage
The stillness with a sound
Of its own making.

Outside the paper room
The children in the playground kill
The summer with their cries.
I look out at the sunny hill
Of sky, but cannot catch the words they scream
To give their spirits ease.

If I, too, could give a shout
Of fear or pleasure, I could play
Myself into their endless game.
But I stand outside their day.
The dumb words are fastened in my throat,
And will not come.

Amour de Tête

A warm pallor, dusk
Of the dark head bound
With the brows' black coronet
Hangs like a living mask
Upon the artless memory.
A mouth, its schoolboy roughness
Firm, and smiling on the grains of teeth;
Ears the daylight shines through,
And night crisps with fever;

Nostrils that seem to dream
Their fragrances as shut eyes their colours;
Pupils that stain like faint bruises
Their closed and soot-fringed lids.

— This is your face, that I have looked upon,
Waking and sleeping, so many times.
Lest I might fail, one day, to recollect it,
I write it here, finding it even now
Inscrutable, dying, not to be apprehended.

Wreath Makers: Leeds Market

A cocksure boy in the gloom of the gilded market bends
With blunt fingers a bow of death and the flowers work with him.
They fashion a grave of grass with dead bracken and fine ferns.

An old woman with a mouthful of wires and a clutch of irises
Mourns in perpetual black, and her fists with the sunken rings
Rummage in the fragrant workbasket of a wreath.

A laughing Flora dangles a cross between her thighs
Like a heavy child, feeds it with pale plump lilies, crimson
Roses, wraps it in greenery and whips it with wires.

And here a grieving flower god with a lyre in his arms
Fumbles mute strings in the rough-gentle machine of his fingers,
His eyes wet violets, and in his mouth a last carnation.

Mourners all, they know not why they mourn,
But work, and breathe the perfumes of their trade
(Those flower-voices, through which death more keenly speaks)

With suitable dispassion; though they know their emblems fade,
And they at last must bear a yellowed wreath
That other hands, and other harvesters have made.

Homage to Vaslav Nijinsky

You are that legendary figure, never seen,
   but always glimpsed beyond the dim
dream's transparent backcloth ; or in green

dark groves, the wings of time's topless auditorium
there where at evening the misted lake is laid away
like a remembered silence in the angry day
   you wander, a young and lonely prince,
far from the huntsmen in the magic wood,
      and drawn by sinister enchantments, visions
of a swan that glides and calls across the haunted glade.

You are the rose breathing its own and universal essence,
   the shadow leaping from the body it has understood
into music's air, the pure design of its deliverance
   and pattern of the mind's bare, ordered solitude.
You are both fool and harlequin, capricious, melancholy
dancer at funerals of innocence and love's wise folly.
   You are the loveless, lost, the lonely and the dumb,
the vanquished who alone rehearse what triumphs mean
   the spectre whose reality is our belief; the faun for whom
no curtain falls upon the mystery that he has always known.

After Pentecost

The wonder is that I write
This, when I cannot find a word.
Once everything came to my hand,
The farthest phrases, and the closest calls,
And I drew my meaning lightly
From the waters of a page.

I filled each line
With something more than words,
And kept the spirit moving
Like spring and summer, easily
As birds, or the shadow of wind in leaves
Over the waters of a page.

A bitter season
Of death and parting
Found the heart, that once
Was durable, done,
And the rippling gone
From the waters of a page.

— My fate is still unknown.
I cannot tell if 1
Am well or ill;
The world is far away
That once I mirrored close
Upon the waters of a page.

Yet for the first time now,
As if 1 learned to speak
Again, after a long dumbness,
1 seek the wind of a word.
The wonder is that 1 write
This, upon the waters of a page.

A Visit to Bronteland

The road climbs from the valley past the public
Park and turns, at the Haworth Co-operative Stores,
Into the grey stone village, and the steep
Street leading to the Parsonage, the Inn, the W.C.s;
To the Church of St. Michael and All Angels, high in trees.

The West Lane Baptists are putting on
Patience, the playbills say. The Heathcliffe Tearooms are aglow
With English teachers in sensible tweeds. Bearded cyclists
Lean on their pedals, and their saddles shine and sway
Up the hill to the Y.H.A.

Across the valley thick with mills
The fellside rises like an aerial map
Of fields and drystone walls and farms.

Pylons saunter over with a minimum of fuss,
And round the bend from Keighley comes the Bronte bus.

An arty signboard poses Charlotte in a crinoline
And ringlets, penning, *Jane Eyre*, at a table, with a quill.
This must be it': —The wondering Americans, like Technicolor ads.,
Have reverence plainly written on their open faces.
They know just how one should behave in hallowed places.

A sea of scriptured slabs
Shines in the graveyard under the twilight rain.
The cold winds are crying in the trees.
New heights above the pines
Are wuthered by tractors of open-cast mines.

The church where the Brontes worshipped
Is long demolished. Only a brass plate
Marks where their bones are buried. Smothered
In Parks Committee geraniums, Anne lies alone
In Scarborough Old Churchyard, under a dolled-up stone.

Now, in the village roofs, the television aerial aspires.
No idle toy would have tempted Branwell
From the 'Bull', and brandy; or kept that sister
From her tragic poems. They knew they had nothing but themselves
And the moor. It is we, who want all, who are poor.

The Prodigal Son
For my father, died 21st January 1958

In a cold season you suddenly left our home
When I was far away, and sick in mind.
Those harsh days in my distracted winter
Must have touched you, too, and the heart
That failed you as my own gave up the ghost.
My dark nights blazed with sleepless candles
In my drugged room shuttered tight against the bells,
The stars, the snow, the people thin as burnt-out sticks,
The black and iron-frosted gardens of a city that was once
A living rose of stone, and now was only stone.
The devil took me there, and spoiled my innocence.
I did not know how pure my heart had been
Till then and there, when that fair-faced demon came
With willing smiles and dangerous embraces
To poison me with kisses, and to take my name.

Out of my flowering mouth he sucked my words,
And from my open hands tugged lines of life.
He made me touch a saint's dead bones
With blind fingers that my thoughts had made unholy;
He took away your spirit from my eyes.

I lent myself to evil, thinking it was truth
Beyond all good and ill, beyond
The neat divisions of the body and the soul.
Father, I saw my long delusion, for the grace
He promised me was vain, and never could be yours.
The trouble gathered in the face you knew,
That always changed, from hour to hour,
But now became a fixing mask of grief, the clown's,
A stunned look I shall never tear away.
The devil made me love his cruel gift.

There came that long night of my perjured soul,
The night in which you died, so far away,
As if my absent hell had killed you, too.
In the dead morning, one living thing within me
Was my sadness, that made me dress in black.

I did not know that you were dead,
And yet I dressed in black, to damn the sun
That led my shadow through the rigid town.
I did not know that you were dead;
And yet I bought your flowers, deep carnations.

Father, this was a year of bitter tears.
It seemed I had been weeping always for my fall
From grace, my own sad death, and still
Go weeping with an evil eye, and weep for you
Who left me lost and far away, beyond forgiveness.

I came back, father, to our wintered house,
And saw you lying still and cold and glad,
A mask of mute astonishment upon your face.
I touched your lovely forehead, chill as stones,
And felt beneath my hand the outrage on those other bones.

In San Esteban, beneath the altar, still they lie
In broken peace, a peace I killed, a devil's pledge.
— O, father, let my last touch rest your ashes, love,
And from this sleepless desert drive my devil out:
Let you return, and smile upon your prodigal.

PANAYIOTA KONSTANTOPOULOU

Socrates

I remember Socrates
A dear and funny man.

Tall and stout
Proud yet humble
Mostly dishevelled
But honest and great.

Betrayed, scapegoated,
As history declares
A teacher and philosopher,
A sage for all time.

Clever but never knowing
Always questioning
Alpha and omega,
Well taught and learned.

Tragic and comic by turns
Aristophanes knew little
Ridiculed him in 'The Clouds'.

Dignified he chatted with friends,
The last hours before death
Poison, hemlock, death
Approaching scenes of love'
As final hour approached.

Remember

To feed the spirit
To be content,
Release the muse
For your intent.

Pen a verse
And then another,
Traverse the page
Like a holy father.

Corner the psyche
Of fine words –
Oh Lord
Don't let them be scarce.
A prayer of hope
Like a wishing well,
Churns out words
That on the tongue dwell.

Vibrant and pert,
The mind alert,
The soul wise,
To any disguise.

Let truth and honesty
Be your spirits guides,
Let friendship swell
To the depths of one's eyes.

Hors d'oeuvre

Your eyes feasted upon me
From the first glance
A prime cut to be manipulated
By fingers, mouths, tongues and teeth,
Lips chopping on pieces of dice,
What price for a slice of me?

For you to satiate an appetite
Shallow in the gut
Amuse me with a rebuttal,
Or is that too cultural?

DAVID LAMBERT

Drinking from her Well

I walk an autumn day far beyond the bounds of leisure
questing a route to your well, the stain that names yellow springs
winter is closing in, snuggling a blanket of leaves about the sleeping trees
a redheaded woodpecker checks my every intersecting choice
drumming round each trunk as I dance the axis of our voice

befriending my thirst for miles by carrying it one step at a time
stumbling along a wide path where scattered shadows still hold snow
I am listening inside this calm forest silence for a wet rushing
for memories lost seven years before when my heart tore between two lands
there a wife who would not soften and here a family who could not understand

now only one I am less so for your ephemera alights with every gaze
teaching me to trust my vision you give no form to fix my eyes
as surely as my pen draws these gestures of love from its ink
so do I drink your mystery to represent our passionate play
dreaming delight alive I wake to you at dusk of fall's last day

under ash grey sky we emerge into a clearing cradling an assembly of stones
overwhelmed by the music of water white washing rock we weep a mirror flow
and cup our hands with homecoming to taste and taste and taste again
a sweetness which melts our memories of sadness to the bone
how could I ever have believed we were suffering so alone?

Larkin's Curse

is my own, for we've both been bred to hurt
thus anywhere our eyes may rest is benediction
holding ourselves unheld, anxious over every spurt
what may not look back invites our preferred reflection

times gone by he and I would have frequented temple wells
indulged the indulgence of women whose eyes went deep

then our playful words would have shaped simpler spells
perhaps we might have even learned to weep

but now, right now, men like us are held at bay
our waves too big, our hungers too earthy to be humane
for this vision which shatters facades we pay, we pay
with perversions of privacy that shape in solitude - disdain

yet in that instant when a forever curve reveals
every shadow forsaken ... her skin briefly steels

British Tea for Boston Party

Albion's most powerful icon is neither crown nor sceptre
not the cross, not even the stolen foam-stained pint glass
this land's symbol supreme is a kettle wreathed in steam

parents pace all night with worry as a child's fever rages
when dawn breaks, as does the illness, shoulders sag with calm
no praises on high, no celebration dances, no hugs and tears
just a simple question "shall I put the kettle on?"

lovers quarrelling with gutsy accusations dredging up their bile
discover a need for each other more genuine than fantasy
no passion tears the sheets, no pledges of forever fidelity
just a simple question "shall I put the kettle on?"

friends out of touch thrown back in contact by tragedy
shift awkwardly between social niceties and time's desperation
yet a single gesture can bridge their decade spanning chasm
just a simple question "shall I put the kettle on?"

like your divided nation each expression is crowded with reference
a minefield language where every detonation opens comic potential
in the absence of apologies still one spell salves all wounds
"shall I put the kettle on?" is not a simple question

Let's Write Barry a "White Sound" Open Reply

no question why when my muse moves me so
we greet you here where typography is clear
and the intention is to rend the wind we blow
the wind we share ... poetry

it is late, and my angel sleepless sighs
at my mortality and continued morality
she is conscientious despite her tireless thighs
and insists this convivial reply . .. poetry

she and I, we both have received your words
on fire without fear upon pages held dear
shapes of listening, the stanzas like birds
on a live wire ... poetry

other work is calling now, she tickles my hair
teasing my tenacity to shape the mendacity
of her manifest impossibility, skin invisible fair
she honours you with ... poetry now

NEIL LEADBEATER

The Long Goodbye

Lytes Cary was the last place my father took me to
before he died. Never one for detail,
he took himself off on a tour of his own
through the close-lipped, hedged-in corridor
oblivious to the border.

Although the garden was closed, he'd bought
our way in with politeness and talk of my journey
        south.
For a short time, we had the place to ourselves.

When I saw the silence that settled in his face
I knew I could not share the wonder of the day
or thank him enough for his patience.
He took no interest in it and I had no means
        to bring it back
for his life was nearly over.

My Last Afternoon with Mrs Pennwarden

She was a small woman
with features delicate as bone china.

Next-door sightings were rare.
An occasional glimpse through the high hedge
as she pegged out the Monday wash.

The afternoon we were invited over
I remember the crowded furniture, the half-drawn
curtains that shut out the sun
as if too much light would have rendered her invisible
and how our talk was held in check
when she tuned in to
Sketch Club.

Last afternoons are only remembered long after
        they are gone.
They spread like ripples on the surface of the mind
when that which you hold so close in your grasp
is cast out into the rolling wave
like so many wreaths
at sea.

Somehow we knew
we would not pass that way again.

MIKE LOVEDAY

Rain

I stand beside the crossroads cold feet deep
In sorrow waiting for the clouds to pass;
Umbrella open, rain is dancing round.
The rainfall sings of my mind's misery;
The constant pitter-patter feeds my thoughts.
A heavy shadow spreads across my brow:
The same gravity which drags the drops down,
Keeps me restricted, tied down to fixed ground.
Plunged in sadness I let the umbrella fall.
The rain washes my head, cleanses me with
Sympathetic splash, soaks my skin and soul.
A puddle grows and gathers at my feet;
It seeps into the soles of my old shoes;
Rain nourishes my body tip to toe.
A river forms coursing through the gutter
To a drain; I would flow with that water,
Disappear with my newly washed sorrow
Down into some dark place, be channelled through
Systems out to sea, re-emerge, reborn
As rain to fall and nourish earth somewhere.

21st March 2002

Encounter in the Smoking Room

'A real good carpenter I used to be, I did.
And look at me now.'

Hardened finger prods the sheaf pf papers in his lap:
Referral for Brain Injuries....
I wonder what on earth this means - botched surgery? car crash?
I aim a glance, sympathetic query,
But I miss: Jim's eyes reach away to the distance.

'I've travelled the world - America, France, the Isle of Wight.
I've got two kids.
My family don't visit anymore.
I'm on my own.'

Tamed eyes redden.

Opposite a patient is wracking his body in two,
Throwing his head and chest towards his knees
Like a plank badly sawn in half being worked free.

Jim doesn't notice; on his craggy face I find
Carved heavy lines, a contour map
Of darker journeys travelled by the mind.

I pull out a cigarette and offer one to Jim.
He pockets it, a treasure for safe-keeping, the future.

13th May – 3rd July 2002

DAITHIDH MACEOCHAIDH

Sorrow

The sorrow still seems ever
to survive one's self
in all its deranged extensions,
thrawn and mishappen,
as any Gothic grotesque,
stashed away in an attic,
of one's own;
finding yourself still
with the live and the quick,
slowly swinging from the tether
of your self-wrought noose
to out-laugh the morning
with the sorrow of surviving
one's self.

Still

Storm passes,
I shore up what is left of the head
  Prop up some doll, figure of person
to send back out there, to discover,
    to identify remains, as the cracks
    in the wall, spread and splinter
    to the sound of breaking bone,
    I find a shade of quiet enough to capture
    a sense of still ... a fractured
moment where the great shout
of the brain is frozen,
mid-grimace, caught almost
smiling, as winds quicken.

ANNA MENMUIR

Love for Sale

Nike's selling love today
the cool sporty kind
in silver, black and grey
high support insoles you'll find

The hotter kind is for the night
Top of the range with
flashing heels to light
your way to next week's rave

They're selling love for men - hard
with scientific promises of
high performance and toe guard
all-inclusive in the price

They're selling love for women too,
pink dreams with power
sockless glories in a shoe
air-sprung high for look-down glower

At passers-by untrained by Nike
brown slip-ons are enough
a relic-of-a-rhyme, tapping
song, "can't buy me love".

RICHARD MIDDLEBROOK

Final Intellectuals

Intellectuals, they are not now as they were,
Their world retreats, final shadows fall,
The fight is over, heavy eyelids trail in the dust.

Sunset is here and the East must solemnly wait,
Cool eyed thinkers stir in the dusk,
Literature wanes, the western chill waxes.

Who can point now and say, there's a fool!
All pass under one common roof,
There are no meals served now.

Only the vain empty clattering of plates;
There are no striving spirits,
The world is lost in a Trappist debate.

There burns no intellectual energy for glorious things,
The thinker lies with eyes askance;
The cold-footed Gods have come upon the scene.

The Call of the Goddess

Teach me if you will the song of the wood,
Of long ago when the rose-hue was on the world;
Pale Reason is my craft and that has failed,
May has come and gone, her season unfurled.

And Daisies like silver children of the unchained Moon
Have trembled their blithe feet on the green
And the world basks in summer's warm swoon
And from strong skies has trembled a breeze unseen.
Teach me if you will the ways of wild woman wisdom,
Land of the skies, and alleyways of the sunlit wood,
Like lines in some verse of intricate freedom
Where a world reveals itself out of Holy Womanhood.

I Spent this Afternoon

I spent this afternoon reading modern poetry,
Draining the waters from dirty ditches,
Being scratched by harpy wings
And finding "logic", arranged in a pattern
And hearing madmen justify madness,
 No life just puppet strings.

Queen of Swords

The cruel queen! With whip and goad in hand
Garbed in black! You are Death's infernal mistress!
Your beauty is peerless, in you nothing is bland,
You rule over Life, its bloodstained priestess!

Queen of Cups

Lost queen forever in Reflection
Your magic is of the still pool
Though many accuse you of introspection
Your simple brilliance is to be cool.

MAROUSHKA MONRO

Seasonal Affective Disorder

Morning.
The sky's greyness invades my room -
a stealthy enemy.
Clouds surround me
their misery grounding me
rendering me immobile.

I feel sad, gloomy, full of despair -
I stare at the window
willing some light to brighten my mood.

I wonder if I suffer from SAD
a seasonal deficiency I'm told
sold to us as a reasonable label
for unstable, unbearable moods
which affect those in the bleakness of winter
giving them an impression
a taste
of all year - round depression.

The cure is a dose of artificial sunlight
emanating the brightness of summer
the glimmer of sun and hope
no drugs or ECT required
to inspire SAD people back to sanity.

Otherwise a trip to Benidorm will do.
Beach mats and a 'chill out' T-shirt
squirting suncream
screening away the UVA's
feeding yourself sunlight
fighting away the blues.

But what about the sad all-year rounders
who flounder even when the light
brightly floods through their windows
mocking in May and June
taunting on a bright summer's day.

The brightness just serves
to shatter your nerves.
You wish it was dull and grey
so you'd have some excuse...
instead of feeling mad in Summer
you could simply say you're sad in Winter.
That would explain
the pain
confusion
delusions
illusions
all life's contradictions.

Yes, on a bright day like today
I think of Shakespeare's words:
'but thou eternal summer shall not fade'
and I wish I could say
look at me!
I'm not depressed
mad or low.
SAD is my diagnosis
the prognosis is good.

Come summer I'll be drunk with sunshine
elated
understood.

I Need to Know

When you leave
please don't close the door
leave it slightly ajar
(never slam it)
I need to know where you are.

Whistle as you walk down the street
clap your hands
or tap your feet.
Call out:
'See you soon!'
for all to hear
it may help to calm my fear.

There's something in the act of closing my door
which brings back distant memories
I'd rather forget.
I know it must seem insecure...
or even a downright bore
knowing this simple gesture
makes me feel nervous, anxious and fret.

Even so...
When you go home
leave my door slightly ajar
(never slam it)
whistle down the wind...
it's as if it's been given the run of the place.
Yes, the house seems a curious thing.

The Lighting of Fires

As imperceptibly as grief
the summer lapsed away

Yet is it only summers' loss
that autumn comes to ease?
Like some magician's hand,
it conjures and deceives.

Slowly as they turn, once
green and dewy leaves,
so slowly do they start
to burn. Before the cold

undressing of the trees,
they'll glow. Staked down
to hardening ground, these
beacons are to warn of winter.

JIM MOORE

At the 'Candles for the Holy Souls'

You're a column, or a tower -
churchless, but of spiritual design.
Tilted to the kiss of another,
you are betrayed.
Condemned, I spike you on the hill.

You well up. Until you're
spilling tears for blood.
Life flickers back and forth
but you die.

I imagine it,
but only in a dream,
you rising up again,
your light re-appearing in the world.

The House and the Four Rogues

The house seems a curious thing
as it befriends the slip earth upon the hillside.
The cold north wind is let in
to make an acquaintance with fire.
While water, that most cunning
and pernicious of all the elements,
just comes and goes throughout;

ALAN MORRISON

The Rosary Beads

Dour Miss Wall casts dark on our
pale foreheads, fingers the rosary beads,
makes us chant a Hail Mary
for the rub of every wooden ball –
morning instruction in future obsession
at English Martyrs Primary School.

9 'o'clock cold polished floor
grounds our numbers' numb bums in
an overcast assembly hall;
Calvary clouds crowd the windows;
the dark jackdaws like a flock of crows.

Morning has broken...

pince-nez pinched, beak-nosed Miss Blades
perches like Professor Yaffle
at her wood bookend piano,
marches thimble fingers on
the thumping ivories...

He's got the whole world in his hands...

one hundred and something O-shaped mouths
chorus OHP-penned cant:

Do not be afraid...

The music dies; lift of spirits
sinks to sighs.

Miss Wall re-manifests, impresses
guilt, our holy catechism –
without speaking issues this instruction:

Question your desires.

My eyes restrain tears.

My thoughts leap back.
Each bead sticks in my throat,
imagining Hell's fires...

The Glove Compartment

In the thrumming back of the car
my legs cramped by bagfuls of things
mother's stashed here for fear of swallowing,
I help her focus from the back seat,
her saner side, shut off with the powdered
glucose sweets in the glove compartment.
My eyes cast back to the bags at my feet.
She throws a panda-eyed stare
from the dark rear-view mirror.

Through the smudged windscreen my mock
composure shivers with leafless trees
twisting in the wind. Stark markers
for my probing on limits of time;
waning strength; deathly sky.
I'm lost in myself for grim minutes;
struggle to trace true bouts of substance
in outlines of thought-shaped clouds.

Mother Mouse

My tiny mother in her tiny kitchen
Rinsing the washing up –
A poem warped above the sink
Entitled *Don't Give Up*.

But Greeting Card wise pearls aside,
Sentiments tire now;
Thirty-five years she's survived
Each wrung-out wedding vow.

For better, for worse, for richer, for poorer,
A shine for bees-wing eyes –
A sud-filled cup for a moment's doubt –
Some sparkle for disguise.

She scurries around her mental wheel
Like an obsessing mouse,
Spins her chores like effortless confessions;
Swallows her sobs as she tidies the house.

Death's Breathtaking View

We clutch the threads that stitch our seamless lives
Immersed in glass routines like black shark eyes;
A sentence hanging over all our heads;
The grimace of a clock face offering
No other explanation but its ticking;
A faceless wall at the foot of our beds.
All we can be sure of is powerless doubt
And the door we came in will invite us out
To nonsensical oblivion or bliss;
Or a frozen limbo while turning the bend.
So we burn the candle at both ends.
In the meantime all we scrimp is this:

Faith in the *soul*, a light that leads us on
Through the dark to terrifying perfection –
Anything but nothing, to be lost in the night,
The pitch-white mist of a fog-bound sea,
The unthinkable smallness of eternity –
Anything but the turning off of lights.

Some seek solutions in the superstitious;
Gregarious others simply drink like fish
Clinking glasses they can't see through –
Salvation: saliva of the garrulous.
Perhaps the only sanity is madness
When comprehending death's breathtaking view.

Some take the plunge, pre-empt the sea;
In spite of being contradictory,
Cancel dark with dark. Obviate
The inevitable? Impossible; we know
All we've come to love one day has to go –
But what could be more morbid than to wait

Until the darkness swallows us? And yet
No sense in stubbing out lit cigarettes;
Best to leave just ashes for the ashtray;
To try and come to terms long in advance;
Stretch perception of deceptive distance;
Put off the problem for an umpteenth day.

Miss Discombobulated

Wearing laundry of years, two holes
for eyes where blackbirds pecked the linen
lined with experience's permanent creases,
she clung to the word 'discombobulated'
as if a thick, warm, comfortable fur-coat;
trampled years since contented
with hyperbole of 'moments' reeking like
cheap white wine in a lukewarm glass;
her past, a fug of pub fag-smoke
perfuming her black Hispanic hair;
ages since pages she once wrote
saw shimmer of day; memories'
invisible walls stalled her everywhere.

Intrusive Thoughts

Outnumbered by invisible bullies
punching at my equilibrium,
bruising with intrusive thoughts,
I despaired (can't think of a better word)
as I followed the other boys down to
the muddy pitch: scared of stopping
loving my father, though impossible,
it tormented me for frozen moments;
I panicked; couldn't figure it:
numbed by the obsessive buzz
of fear-bees bumping about my head.

PAUL MURPHY

Images

Sound echoes narrowly
On the stairwell:
The night we left the cinema
The homecoming was to a house
Bereft of light
Strangely, sinister,
As if crimes,
Odious, terrible
Had taken place.

In the basement we found a wall
Of flesh and blue,
Don Quixote rode in logic and abstract
The wind pierced the wells
The women of Guernica
Screamed in fixity
Under the house
The paintbrush we castigated
Had changed history.

Stealthily, we crept back
Up the stairs
Left the scene
Undisturbed
In the car again
We returned
Later, we washed
Our hands of history
The artist may take it
And make of it
Our trivial destiny
We live out our irrelevance
Our nullity again and again.

Snow

Snow, unalterably disdaining
On first looking to the sky

Corrosive glance, my unmatched antipathy
What were we comprehending?

Snow, unalterably disdaining
Its never-caring fallingness
Through the vaporous air, cloud bursts
Of breath-taking whiteness
Emblazoned in winter's oppression
Surrounding us with falling momentedness
Grasp the unalterability, passive nullity
Of snow, unalterably disdaining.

Chamber Music

Music from another room
Congeals the mind
Coerces senses
The gentle intercourse
Of string on string
Music of mind, memory
Wasp flits
On the pane. moth to the lamp,
Illumination of past presence
In the shadowed eye
Of the lamp's embrasure,
Hair falling,
On my shoulder
Brown eyes, brown hair
Remembrance
Rain patinas
The hammer clack
Of water on tin
This Saturday's afternoon's
Drudgery
Remembrance
TV set, pools coupon
Struggling for the memory
The dark eyes, hair
The lamplit
Dim places.

S. NETTLE

Doors

Shuffling down this endless corridor,
A thousand exits surround me.
Dream-like opening each in turn;
Dying a little as they reveal to me
A million miles of empty space
Leading to a billion doors.
There must have been a door
Through which you dragged me,
Comatose and disillusioned,
So many years ago.
There must have been a door here in the wall.
Watching me with hardened eyes
You offer no direction, but
Note everything down in your little black book.
Watching and waiting for reactions
In this bleakness;
This mighty expanse of nothingness
Into which I have been mercilessly thrust.
I let you write.
I let you note down your theories and your
Hypotheses
Because I know that there has to be
A door here in the wall.
You let me wander, try every door in turn,
Counting thousands and thousands of minutes away,
Trying every door here in the wall.
You let me wander
Because you know and I know
That we are both safe in the knowledge
That I cannot escape.
There is no door here in the wall.

Walking the Halls

Listlessly treading the halls
Bare feet encased in over-stuffed
Marshmallow slippers.
Swishing through deep-pile carpets;

High on being low.
Tendrils of plush, institutional green
Reach out for her -
Snake-like -
Entwining her in their lush jungle undergrowth.
The calls of wild, bug-eyed animals
Reach her from beneath the treetops;
Calling out, bawling, roaring.
The wails of hunters' quarry
Caught in the trap of her mind.
She closes her eyes and hurries
The last few steps to her door
And she smiles...

CAROLYN O'CONNELL

Manifistations

It is midsummer. In wood and walk
imported sculpture grows in the park.
Piled before the jet altar
bronze nugget offerings temple the lawn.
The iron blue waive crests in the grass
bathing the children.

Out of the bronze egg
laid beneath the chestnut trees
a child's hand emerges, waiving
as the chased tree weeps icy droplets
From the bronze branches in the knot garden
and a fleshless iron horse rides
against the sun; casting no shadow.
Metal boned, the worker strolls forever
along his fallen plinth past
triangular people endlessly climbing thin steps.

Sculpted black as iron the queen of the night
extends her wreath of cast bones
over rosebeds
as the flat bronze sun is caught in steel baskets
and the red tortoises walk towards each other
over the sundial, calibrating time

White

I always remember how you looked
the night I lay sick in your bed.
There were three faces
white with anxiety, concern.

Spheres in front of the linen press
whose open contents clung like ivy to orderly shelves,
that grew white tentacles of sheets,
threw down leaves of linen pillow cases
onto the white slipped floor.

In my pink pyjamas I passed you.
I walked down the white oak staircase,
careful not to knock the four brass candlesticks
on their white ledge beside the banister rail.

I crept unseen into the garden
(where your table lay abandoned
covered by a white lace cloth)
the night grass dampening my feet,
looking up I tried to escape.

I was recalled by the memory
of the white faces of three women
and someone who had held my hand
and knelt at the head of the bed.

Vortex

He was a calm man:
the vortex of the storms
blowing across my growing years;
his stillness wasn't acquiescence,
was the commanding whisper
of a warning wind.

From his calmness came:
the power to survive
tradition's choking winds,
freeing me from all preceding women,
women aroused by beeswax
seduced by rising dust.

WENDY OLIVER

Out of Place

1.

An old whore but a good one
Cumberland Basin Street
For seafaring men only
Engaged her frail lock-gates
Nightly when bulky ships
Crowded from Avonmouth.
I lived a happy year
Watching it all from the window.
Night upon land and river
One dark unbroken meadow
Would bloom with dandlelights,
All known to sense grew there
Odorous and secret, live,
Sliding between the fingers.
As each stilled mast and lamp
That bore its burning head
Filed to the hanging stars
Erased, the horizon slept.

Now dream of the eye's feast
Gorged upon thunderstorms
And replete with Somerset hills
Grow pale, steal out from memory
Or die in the north wind's
Dawn and indifferent teeth.

I am facing up to reality,
I am breathing sulphur dioxide,
Hydrocarbonic carcinogens
Pack down in my red lungs.
I shall die of something genuine,
Industrial like silicosis,
Though not with the hell-mouth bang
That once voided a mine-shaft
Of my Uncle Lewis for one.
His immaculate parlour piano

Is closed, and over his grave
The Bluebells of Scotland lean.

2.

Through hopeless weeping valleys
Through hopeless smiling alleys
Of Great Victorian Clangertown
Behold an ersatz cowboy
Ox-shouldered and ricket-legged
Going some unfathomable way!
His soft demented head
Turns-o come and look-
Slow as a cow's regarding
The arc of a thrown lasso.
O what a sight what a scream
Something to tell the girls!
The thin-drawn blonde on his arm
Guiding his frail enormity
Bows, bows to the effort.

Such love and sickness
A dream past belief
Perfectly confirmed
Is the long-buried heart.

Hold to it, close around it
Flatulent north city
Unbespoke off-the-peg city
Neither cut from green plain
Nor fastening the fleeced hills,
For if you part your flat vowels
What have you to show?

I walk in its centre and weep.
Where it should clamp and beat
Life-blood through urban arteries
It gapes its unmentionable space
Its inborn changeless defect
Caused by no bomb or fire.
Though hands that might mantle bombs
Have lined some soft stone girls

In Belsenite rows, in keeping.
Aloft the assumptive Prince
Petrified in his flurry of horse-gear
Points onward! to the main-line station.

3.

Car hits a road island
Rhode Island Red
On the red road
Both land dead
Boys yell chicken!
Road-sweepers sweep blood.

4.

Miss Cohen the virgin mother
Attended by cherubim
Bestows sugared indulgences
On the steps of the off-licence.
Puffed cheeks both brown and pink
Clamour their loud hosannas
Sung in lingua franca
Of north English slums, late spring.
Friends! Ears to the ground!
What cur on Stonegate Green
Sours the May morning?
Shall we choke it in streamers
Of a suddenly risen maypole
Sprung from the mouth of mayday?
Yes, my old haggard phallus,
Surge with the waiting wind
Deal death to suburban dogs!
Avaunt her holy slippers!
We'll lift her clear in the air
And carry her high to her throne
And give her John Barleycorn's crown,
Miss Cohen is queen of the may!

5.

Yet all gives way at last,
Maypole and maybranch fall,

The delicate lock-gates snap.
Fire mines the mine-shaft.
All aches with inbuilt faults:
The mind's groin is ruptured,
Even the mind that thinks it.

We love, and lose later,
Or lose sooner, or never love at all.
And still lose.
That which would root and grow
Is always out of place:
The malcontent, the inborn
Fault through which we evolve.
Neither on pleasure nor endurance
Does it find foundation.
In a tent, in an unfamiliar land,
Here in my own words
Is my only home.

Spell-breaking

This is the junk-market
Where all my dreams have been
Doing secret trade. I recognize
Tile-shards like those I found
In childhood fresh-bombed ruins
Still coloured, and childhood dreams.
Here an abandoned corset
One shoe and a brown goatskin
Are wrapped round rubble,
'Come away' you say 'I fear it'
As I do in the dream, when I am alone.
But did I ever see in sleeping
Journeys through slum-clearance
That-like a devil's war-engine
To besiege the sane skull-
Five stone steps that mount

To a bricked-up doorway, no going through
Even as a ghost?

Magenta rosebay willowherb

Drugs me with weed-scent, how velvet the
    bricks are!
The trash bright as eye-shadow
Insinuates itself.
Streets of a Roman market
Can have been no narrower
No more cobbled. Stumbling
We've almost ended the inevitable
Crossing of wasteland
Unscathed by thicketty bush-thistles,
    bed-spring foot-traps.
Approaching the highway, lifting your face
    to the full-lit
Theatre of sky 'How beautiful!' you say.
But in the lead-clouded back-stage still I sense
As if in sleep, whoever stands in waiting
With cold breath and with aah! black wings.

An End of Winter Night

Pavements of Cambridge, whetstone under frost,
Sharpened her steps on alleys and arcades.
Back of Magdalene the river was standing stiff
As a new-pressed Ackerman print, tree-copperplated.
And in King's College chapel stalactites
And stalagmites of stone
Made a tremendous cavern where her whispers
Turned from mist to icicles.
Lodging that night was hard to find and cold
Under one blanket and a fraying coat,
But life was inside her-the beginning of one-
And she was glad it held its own still heat
With no help from the weather or the bed.
It seemed that in a well-upholstered season
She would have slept insensible
Of that internal constant generating,
But here she was and gradually grew warm
And warm enough to sleep.
By morning the room glowed, and when she left it
She stepped on shining pavements, heard the river
Shifting among its broken shell, and the organ
Warning the shaking buttresses of King's
That cold Clare Hall was melting in the sun.

HELEN OVERELL

Necklace

we sat in limbo in the long grass
child minds brimful of time in bodies
buoyant with full grown ease - you were still,
calm, a pool of silence deep and clear
as far off cobalt skies filled with clouds
of almond blossom, your lineage
bold as a Persian miniature

your minder, diminutive, white haired,
kept watch close by, starched uniform - blue
as an ocean of cornflowers edged
with a cirrus of lace - startling
in the green field, hands trammelled with age
buffing silver to buckled brightness,
marking time with a silent strathspey

my mind floated, clusters of star drift
daisies grew all around, my fingers
gathered and threaded a gold freckled
garland for me and a long loose chain
for you but you shrank back, fended off
my gift, paused a moment for thought and
then showed me your necklace of rope burns

your guardian wove words to a dove
gray shawl of comfort for your shaking
shoulders and pushed the thought of you limp
as a rag doll through a lengthening
lens until we stood without tremor
your lithe limbs warm as your gentle smile
my hands clutching the wraith of a wreath

MARIO PETRUCCI

Mr Haynes

How could we predict that moment
twelve full minutes into his clockwork timetable
with someone burbling he must have died or

something when his door swung open
to frame him plainly not hearing Chesterfield
relax those stupid twangs of ruler as we primed

for the usual bollocking for gathering noise
like an incoming storm - but he simply walked
quarter-speed behind an invisible train of thoughts

stood before us scanning the benchtops
as though seeking there the one impossible star
in his pupils' faulty instruments that were

shot through with black oil while his face
resonated in all its parts to some distant force
bottom lip hued suddenly with petroleum

and all his precious laws on the brink
in the way that middle button of his labcoat
had been left undone as he nearly almost not quite

breathed some great word into that
distilled void his shaking had made and
the purity of the empty blackboard remained

behind him like a window onto the last night
of the world and our classroom became a space
lightened as if by a wind-felled tree because

Mr Hayes had walked in and walked out again
leaving us to teach ourselves and speculate
that dark vein he laid between two bright lessons

RAZZ

Dear God

Do you look like Charlton Heston
In those epics on the telly
Or are you like those statues
Of the Buddha with the belly

Did you really make the stars
Have you got a face at all
Is planet earth your masterpiece
Do you hear us when we call

Is there hell and is there heaven
Or is that all just in our minds
Do we live a thousand lifetimes
Or is this the only time

That we get to tread a planet
Get to touch and think and feel
Then are we gone forever
Or do we get a better deal

And have you got a sense of humour
When we do the things we do
Do you laugh at all our efforts
To make some sense of you

Are you a beacon of compassion
Or are you made of sterner stuff
Do you like it when some mortal
Attempts to call your bluff

And could you do without disciples
When they come on so fanatical
Have you left it up to us now
And gone on a sabbatical

Are you really just an absence
We project on all the time
Or are you a reality
That goes way beyond the mind

And all those politicians
They must really piss you off
Sundays in the chapel -Mondays
Noses in the trough

And all those Popes and Ayatollahs
Are they just signs of our Soul disease
And are you really only happy
When we're down upon our knees

And who is it I'm talking to
At whom do I raise my fist
I'm sure you're more like energy
Than an Evangelist

And forgive me for these questions
But a small part of the list
Of things I'm mulling over
To see if you exist
And if this is your masterpiece
And if this is your turf
Don't you get frustrated
That we don't know what its worth

And if this is your masterpiece
And if this is your turf
Are you sharpening up the lightning bolts
Before we make it worse

Famine, Hood and Geri Halliwell
Are they precursors of your curse?

GERALD RYAN

Faith

Do you know the demon called death?
Has he visited you in your dreams?
Your waking hours filled, with
Malicious, persuasive, exhortations?
He is a dangerous enemy.
Invisible, inaudible, untouchable,
An unrelenting thought
Planted in your brain,
Like some misplaced genetic fragment.
Out of control,
Displacing, choking, happier thought.
Happy memories become twisted
As in a magic mirror
Distorted, demented shapes of that which
Once they were.
Words of faith and hope forgotten,
Replaced by those which bring only despair.
Yet I am grown angry with this demon.
I am a man,
A good man,
A man for whom I have respect.
No matter what the price,
No matter how lonely the road,
1 must and will fight on.
For to submit to the Demon,
Is to say I am not a man,
And that I refuse to say
   29th May 2003

JOHN S. SAVAGE

The Angel has Grown Tired

The angel has grown tired
she's curled up in the chair
left her harp on the floor
her wings hanging from the door.
she looks almost human

If heaven has forgotten her
and god's doors have closed
I have a room lying empty
since Saint Veronica left.

I put out the light
and the angel is lost in gloom
but as I close the door
I hear a muttered prayer.

I lie awake through the night
listening for her footsteps leaving
but the angel does not move
as dawn's hand gives me hope.

In the morning she is quiet
as she gathers her belongings
and I find myself smiling
as she places them in a locked drawer

DOLLY SEN

Queue

Dinner queue in the psych ward
I'm stuck between two Jesuses
I can see they're both contemplating
feeding the five thousand by doing a
miracle of multiplication with the
rubbery macaroni cheese
A schizophrenic soul abuses
any god that is listening
The catatonic philosophises
with empty words
The anorexic looks down her
nose at us for indulging in
the depravity of sustenance
Why am I here?
Reality, sanity is a book of
lies, I've lost my page
I've become celestially illiterate
Because I know the ending - no
happily ever after
just lonely death
following
a life
that is just a queue
waiting, waiting
for the
madness to end

JON SILKIN

Death of a Son
(who died in a mental hospital aged one)

Something has ceased to come along with me.
Something like a person: something very like one.
And there was no nobility in it
Or anything like that.

Something was there like a one year
Old house, dumb as stone. While the near buildings
Sang like birds and laughed
Understanding the pact

They were to have with silence. But he
Neither sang nor laughed. He did not bless silence
Like bread, with words.
He did not forsake silence.

But rather, like a house in mourning
Kept the eye turned in to watch the silence while
The other houses like birds
Sang around him.

And the breathing silence neither
Moved nor was still.

I have seen stones: I have seen brick
But this house was made up of neither bricks nor stone
But a house of flesh and blood
With flesh of stone
And bricks for blood. A house
Of stones and blood in breathing silence with the other
Birds singing crazy on its chimneys.
But this was silence,

This was something else, this was
Hearing and speaking though he was a house drawn
Into silence, this was
Something religious in his silence,

　　　　Something shining in his quiet,
This was different this was altogether something else:
　　　Though he never spoke, this
　　　　　　Was something to do with death.

　　　And then slowly the eye stopped looking
Inward. The silence rose and became still.
The look turned to the outer place and stopped,
　　　　With the birds still shrilling around him.
　　　　　And as if he could speak

He turned over on his side with his one year
Red as a wound
He turned over as if he could be sorry for this
And out of his eyes two great tears rolled, like stones,
　　　And he died.

To My Friends

It does not matter she never knew
Who Pater was. What is rare
Despite the encirclements of marriage
Or even the political relationships
Affianced beyond parliament
Is love, which breaks the breads.
The staff of women, the dread,
The hunger of men, it is not
Just what I am capable of
If mature; it is the force
Behind those intimations of our senses
progenitor to more growth,
If anything is. Remember,
The moulds of rock perish,
The flower so delicately formed
The minute exactness seems meant
To last. What does live
In the complex fabrics of air,
Uncoloured, and always nubile,
Is this man-like attribute.
So very carefully
Consider what you do
As an action related always

To this eternal motion
In man's leathery breast;
For the way we treat each other
In private is, minutely,
The way we deal with wives
And they their men. Even stones
Wrinkled in a contempt
Of their manipulators
Lie in some comradeship,
For their sakes. And for Man,
Men matter, whether that God
Who made us, and the stones,
Is watching us, or bored
With human agony
Lies in immortal sleep
Terribly locked, not witnessing
The outrages of human hunger
Bearable only because
They must be, even these uptorn
Grains of love that are burned
In complex and primitive agonies
In concentration camps.

Furnished Lives

      I have been walking today
Where the sour children of London's poor sleep
      Pressed close to the unfrosted glare,
Torment lying closed in tenement,
      Of the clay fire; I
Have watched their whispering souls fly straight to God:

      "O Lord, please give to us
A dinner-service, austere, yet gay: like snow
      When swans are on it; Bird,
Unfold your wings until like a white smile
      You fill this mid-white room."
I have balanced myself on the meagre Strand where

      Each man and woman turn,
On the deliberate hour of the cock
      As if two new risen souls,

Through the cragged landscape in each other's eyes.
        But where lover upon lover
Should meet - where sheet, and pillow, and eiderdown

        Should frolic and breathe
As dolphins on the stylized crown of the sea
        Their pale cerements lie.
They tread with chocolate souls and paper hands,
        They walk into that room
Your gay and daffodil smile has never seen:

        Not to love's pleasant feast
They go, in the mutations of the night,
        But to their humiliations
Paled as a swan's dead feather scorched in the sun.
        I have been walking today
Among the newly paper-crowned, among those

        Whose casual, paper body
Is crushed between fate's fingers and the platter;
        But Sir, their perpetual fire
Was not stubbed out, folded on brass or stone
        Extinguished in the dark,
But burns with the drear dampness of cut flowers.

        I cannot hear their piped
Cry. These souls have no players. They have resigned
        The vivid performance of their world.
        And your world, Lord,
                Has now become
Like a dumb winter show, held in one room,

        Which must now reek of age
Before you have retouched its lips with such straight fire
        As through your stony earth
Burns with ferocious tears in the world's eyes:
Church-stone, door-knocker and polished railway lines
        Move in their separate dumb way
                So why not these lives:
I ask you often, but you never say?

The Return

        I have carried for five years
In me, your country cupped with oval leaves.
          It is a land quickened with streams
Which have no confluence, yet they now firmly flow
              One liquid star in my blood;
It is as a jewel there. It is fearful and

         Strange to attend you
For I once fled through your pattern, I who now cup
           Your shape in my palm, and I
Burst from the green veins of your delicate country
             Move into the grey
Borders of the town who crouches in her shadows.

         I revisit you now and find
There is nothing changed in you but myself, I am
            Like a bird
That lightly perches on the angular
              Chimneys of London; I see
The sour hands of that woman folded into her lap.

         And I divine I now shall
Not be admitted easily to your source.
          That image of your streams met in me -
As the confluence of the stars meets in the one eye -
           This I got when I saw
The white shoulder of your profound hill. You were

         Then simple to me, but my thought
That now so distorts you, helped by the sensual flesh
          That exudes its particular scent
The scent that the flesh gives out, and the flower exudes
           As they are loved - the gesture
Of the heart and the movement of the flower are the
            Same -

         That starlike thought of you
Still treads through my head as a dream treads, quietly
          And with precision,
Unendingly real because impossible;
          That thought and that image of you

You now deny. I am refused by you.

        There are a thousand stones in
The shallows of the Avon but must I tender them,
        Become again the intimates of
Your intimates before I begin where you
        Began? The days
Shadow has lengthened and the red sun stirring

        Its more recent beams, in the evening
Grinds up its heat still; and in between the sheltering
        Walls of the town
where the poor's tears are dropped without the leaf
        For their comfort or even
The stalk for their pity, it pierces. May I attend

These stones, as tears should be
Tendered. Say if you will admit me although
        My image of you is false.
Then your jewels, flat and poor, will have my tenderness;
        I will become their friend
Who fold over and over the fragile white rounds
        Of your demanding country.

Respectabilities

Many liberals don't just
Make love, they first ask each other;
And either is free to decline
What the other wishes;
That is, unmitigated
Possession of the beloved's flesh.
Nothing hasty, nothing unconsidered
Catches the liberal by
The hairs of lust. Nothing.
And this consideration
For those feelings
Of the approached one naked
In love or in hunger
Is extended to all.
He will, for instance, ask
A starving man if he

Would eat, pressing
For the particulars
Of hunger. And enquire
Why he is deficient
In bread. All men are treated
With such perception as stones
Get in subjection to
Their shaper, as their use fits
To his. Men are chosen to meet
That judged compassion which
A liberal has. A wounded man
Receives the ointments of love
From matrons, with respect.
Sex, the inhuman hunger,
Demands courteous
Submission, polite domination.
In fact, the turning world,
A stone delicately
Veined with acceptable
Colours, deficient just because
Another stone has gouged
A bit from its flesh
Demands the liberal heart;
Though another stone
Brutal in the untamed
Components - a misshapen
Tongue of useless rock -
Merits, and gets
A frank dismissal.
And this, too, is fair;
Though more than half the earth
Is denied purchase on
That delicate conscience
Cash gives: a fair if privileged
Mind veined with gold.

JAMES SIMMONS

from Memorials of a Tour in Yorkshire

I think this student is called Jane
who leans against me in the booth,
her lips wet with the dirty rain
of Leeds. The flattery of youth
is pleasing to an aging poet who
is waiting for his trunk call to go through.

I am watching the wet fields and hills
to the English coast and the cold sea
and so on till my own phone trills
at home, and then a bit of irony:
'A Mr So-and-so,' as operators say,
'is calling from Leeds, and wishes you to pay.'

Jane winks and kisses me, I hear
my daughter, then my wife says, 'Yes.'
As though my lips were at her ear
I tell her of that night's success
and who I met, honestly trying
 to share my work; but I am lying.

The wife asks, 'Are you alone?'
(Her silly irrelevant instinct to which
she has no right!) 'YES.' When the phone
is dead at last I pity the poor bitch
who's ruined my evening, stick out my tongue
at myself in the mirror: 'Was ever your heart
wrung?'

The Dawning of the Day

Rest easy William Cobbet,
rest easy, William Blake,
and you, wise, gay Lord Byron
who died for freedom's sake.
Rest easy Edward Thomas.
You all have taught the way.

You lived and died to see and speed
the dawning of the day.

Your stubborn courage, Thomas Hardy,
only seemed too mild.
Your lovely jokes were not in vain,
rest easy, Oscar Wilde.
Rest easy D H Lawrence,
for you wore yourself away
to spark the fire of life and speed
the dawning of the day.

Rest easy Patrick Kavanagh
and Myles Nagcopaleen,
your restless bitchy passions
befit the Irish scene
no less than those of Joyce
although he moved so far away.
By devious ways you serve and speed
the dawning of the day.

Rest easy in your bitterness
in Ulster now, MacNeice.
Caged by the easy BBC,
pneumonia was release.
That consciousness of failure
is useful in its way:
the lies of compromise impede
the dawning of the day.

Rest easy Dylan Thomas,
rest easy Geoffrey Hill
(perhaps I shouldn't mention you -
they say you're living still.
But that's no fault of yours.)
We living poets, still at play,
remember you, and memory speeds
the dawning of the day.

Flight of the Earls Now Leaving

I hear that Ormsby will be leaving soon.
That only leaves me, Longley and Muldoon.
Such pillars of establishment, we three;
New University, Arts Council, BBC.
The famous nest of singing birds has flown
across the border or across the foam.
Mahon was too fastidious for Belfast,
he fled to Dublin, but that didn't last,
onward and upward, the ambitious rogue
rests now in London, on the staff of *Vogue*.
And Heaney's skulking in some quaint retreat
in Wicklow or at large in Baggot Street,
drinking with editors in Dublin bars
far from his students and his seminars.
And Leitch, who all things but himself did know?
Across the water, on the radio,
he works his way from crisis into crisis
confounding my attacks by winning prizes.
Hard-biting Michael Foley, the RC
who edited the HU after me
teaches in London Convent schools. The fear
of God still cows the pupils, teaching's easier.
John Montague has been away so long
we hardly miss him. Did he once belong?
America, then Paris, and now Cork,
where the tired Muse is hen-pecked by the stork.

God, I forgot one, and I knew I'd do it -
the daddy of us all, good old John Hewitt
who left before, his reasons being the best,
and came back in retirement to unrest.
I'm left forlorn to do the Gaelic bit,
'to hit and run and howl when I am hit,'
to whine and snivel and lament and moan
our right to be exploited by our own
for which so many Irishmen have died
from the Post Office to the Waterside.
Bards drive with good success across the Border
where all agree the stout's in better order.
How can I blame them, how can I defend

our quixotry who stick it to the end,
comparing their good fortune being away
with their sad impotence if they should stay?

Yet in their going we have lost a host
of men that muddled Ulster needed most.
Daily there grows about us the sad rout
of men that any land could do without:
Wee Brian, the leader of the Planter Stock
who has 'more faces that the Guildhall Clock,'
Big Ian who can bluster, joke and rant,
ignorantly flattering the ignorant,
wet liberals, reformed republicans,
old freedom killers and new Black and Tans.
We four still cherish novels, poems and plays -
outside mad dogs infest the public ways.

A Jig for Seamus

Hear him on the radio
eulogising Sweeney.
The King of Rasharkin
is our Seamus Heaney,
anguished, tormented,
blushing with his prize,
the tongue of the land itself
telling huge lies.

Pickled in the Faber bottle,
in the Guinness curled,
syllables through bog water
bubble to the world.

Lear in a Volkswagen,
Hamlet on TV,
neither an informer
nor an internee.
Green leaf in springtime,
winter, black weeds,
Heaney the chameleon,
blue jeans to tweeds.
Mind in the winter grass

now the sap flows,
body at the fireside
toasting wet toes.

Seek him in the boardroom,
in the backyard,
green shamrock, three in one,
damned elusive bard.
Holding up the art world
of Ireland, arms aching,
instep on home ground,
bogland, quaking.
Antaeus is beckoning
from mother Ireland's quim
to Yeats, Synge, old Lady
Gregory and him.

My Friend the Famous Poet

'But first possess his books. Without them
He's but a sot as I am, nor hath not
One spirit to command.'
Caliban

His is more a library than a mind.
I poke about my own head to find
words that I've seen catch fire
in friction in a phrase. I prefer
well-handled words I can use,
that have been used on me in crowds and queues.

He has to feel the Odeons sell
tickets to damned souls, that Dante's Hell
is in that red-plush darkness. May be his way
is true enough. It's not for me to say.
I feel an eejit pointing parallels
when nothing in those supernatural hells
is half as scary as plain loneliness,
cowardice, jealousy. The skill seems frivolous
that helps men to avert their eyes
from this and that towards hypotheses.

Like Faust he's sold on magic and great whores,
and for his satisfaction many doors
swing open into nothingness. My life
is limited and actual like man and wife.

Geoffrey Hill

'I must conserve myself,' said Geoffrey Hill,
'And husband nature's riches from expense,
submitting to the tyranny of will
and not the mob votes of experience.'
I said, 'I'm marked by the democracy
Of every-man-I-meet's demands. I'm loath
to step back from the common destiny.

I am a wild flower, you're a hothouse growth.
I feel the buffets of the rain, the touch
of healing sunlight in the random hours,
what dies I drop, what flutters past I clutch.'
'Yes,' Geoffrey said, 'but I don't like wild flowers,
although I grant you death takes wild and tame,
festering weeds and lilies smell the same.'

Poor Tom

I suppose when I have the choice
I keep out of his way,
the dark suit and commanding voice
glimpsed in the lavatory
swilling gin from the hip,
kidding himself, not me.
'Give the order, abandon ship,
eh, Jim? Did anyone see?
No, I rather think
not. Feel like a drink?'

Ex-officer material, with almost
perfect formal salutes,
intensely, personally arguing
tactics with colonels or recruits.
With him swanky hotels

seem shelters to crouch in.
Without intimacy he reveals
secrets, blots the escutcheon.
Nothing is too small to sweat after
or too sad for his loud joyless laughter.

In spite of the sudden beauty
in things he says he doesn't know
we only endure him out of pity,
for we know whom we follow,
what is imaginary and what real.
He strides towards the firing
expecting nevertheless a decent meal
and wine, to spill, sensationally boring.
Why must exploding air
flutter his shoulders everywhere?

With evidence of a clear case
We'd court-martial the man
for not knowing his place,
for subversive doubts. He never can
remember what others say
which is insulting. 'Hello soldier,'
he shouts, and one follows his eyes away
over one's own shoulder.
Off to the loo then with some excuse
for a slug of the old juniper juice.

The Rat Under The Roses

My daughter says, 'Don't smoke, Daddy.
It frightens me.' I love that young lady;

but how can I curb my pleasure, be suddenly stealthy
with life, given I'm still strong and healthy?

The stale air gathered in each good lung
resonates on the vocal chords. Anna's fright
is part of a puritan fashion that I must fight
with words and music. These good songs will be sung.

We sing, 'The rat under the roses', and Ben's joke
is to search the bushes. I smile and smoke.

The Road to Clonbarra

Boulders and heather at my shoulder,
below the stoney bridge was narrow,
above I glimpsed the moonlight smoulder
the night we crossed the Owencarrow.

I took the road map from its folder
and kissed my wife, 'Goodbye to sorrow.
Bold we have been and will be bolder
now we have crossed the Owencarrow.'

Old Muckish, beyond rocks and heather,
loomed. We would wake at home tomorrow.
Look for the bleak house mined by weather
then right. Is that the Owencarrow?

'What of the Council of Belfast now?'
'Like the old sow who eats her farrow,'
she laughed. 'We're free of them at last now.
Tonight we've crossed the Owencarrow.'

Like Garibaldi we've surged North,
not Southward like the men from Jarrow.
We knew what charity was worth
before we crossed the Owencarrow.
We sang what had been cramped within us,
neighbours brought whiskey in a barrow
with sandwiches and wines and Guinness
that night we crossed the Owencarrow.

We've burnt our boats and built our dwelling,
drawn the good bow, released the arrow.
Plant trees for shelter, flowers for smelling,
new born beyond the Owencarrow.

STEVIE SMITH

Not Waving but Drowning

Nobody heard him, the dead man,
But still he lay moaning:
I was much further out than you thought
And not waving but drowning.

Poor chap, he always loved larking
And now he's dead
It must have been too cold for him his heart gave way,
They said.

Oh, no no no, it was too cold always
(Still the dead one lay moaning)
I was much too far out all my life
And not waving but drowning.

The Suburban Classes

There is far too much of the suburban classes
Spiritually not geographically speaking. They're asses.
Menacing the greatness of our beloved England, they lie .
Propagating their kind in an eight-roomed style.
Now I have a plan which I will enfold
(There's this to be said for them, they do as they're told)
Then tell them their country's in mortal peril
They believed it before and again will not cavil
Put it in caption form firm and slick
If they see it in print it is bound to stick:
'Your King and your Country need you Dead'
You see the idea? Well, let it spread.
Have a suitable drug under string and label
Free for every Registered Reader's table.
For the rest of me gang who are not patriotic
I've another appeal they'll discover hypnotic:
Tell them it's smart to be dead and won't hurt
And they'll gobble up drug as they gobble up dirt.

W. D. SNODGRASS

From Heart's Needle
for Cynthia

1.

Late April and you are three; today
             We dug your garden in the yard.
      To curb the damage of your play,
Strange dogs at night and the moles tunnelling,
             Four slender sticks of lath stand guard
        Uplifting their thin string.

So you were the first to tramp it down.
             And after the earth was sifted close
      You brought your watering can to drown
All earth *and* us. But these mixed seeds are pressed
          With light loam in their steadfast rows.
             Child, we've done our best.

Someone will have to weed and spread
             The young sprouts. Sprinkle them in the hour
      When shadow falls across their bed.
You should try to look at them every day
          Because when they come to full flower
             I will be off away.

2.

          No one can tell you why
the season will not wait;
         the night I told you I
must leave, you wept a fearful rate
        to stay up late.

          Now that it's turning Fall,
we go to take our walk
           among municipal
flowers, to steal one off its stalk,
        to try and talk.

        We huff like windy giants
scattering with our breath
        grey headed dandelions;
Spring is the cold Wind's aftermath.
        The poet saith.

        But the asters, too, are grey,
ghost-grey. Last night's cold
        is sending on their way
petunias and dwarf marigold,
        hunched sick and old.

        Like nerves caught in a graph,
the morning-glory vines
        frost has erased by half
still crawl over their rigid twines.
        Like broken lines

        of verses I can't make.
In its unravelling loom
        we find a flower to take,
with some late buds that might still bloom,
        back to your room.

        Night comes and the stiff dew.
I'm told a friend's child cried
        because a cricket, who
had minstrelled every night outside
        her window, died.

3.

        Easter has come around
again; the river is rising
        over the thawed ground
and the banksides. When you come you bring
        an egg dyed lavender.
We shout along our bank to hear
our voices returning from the hills to meet us.
        We need the landscape to repeat us.

        You lived on this bank first.

While nine months filled your term, we knew
    how your lungs, immersed
in the womb, miraculously grew
    their useless folds till
terrible air rushed in to fill
them like two shrubs bursting with leaves. You took your
    hour,
caught breath, and cried with your full lung power.

    Over the stagnant bight
we see the hungry bank swallow
    flaunting his free flight
still; we sink in mud to follow
    the killdeer from the grass
    that hides her nest. That March there was
rain; the rivers rose; you could hear killdeers flying
    all night over the mudflats crying.

    You bring back how the red-
winged blackbird shrieked, slapping frail wings,
    diving at my head -
I saw where her tough nest, cradled, swings
    in tall reeds that must sway
    with the winds blowing every way.
If you recall much, you recall this place. You still
    live nearby - on the opposite hill.

    After the sharp windstorm
of July Fourth, all that summer
    through the gentle, warm
afternoons, we heard great chain saws chirr
    like iron locusts. Crews
    of roughneck boys swarmed to cut loose
branches wrenched in the shattering wind, to hack free
    all the torn limbs that could sap the tree.

    In the debris lay
starlings, dead. Near the park's birdrun
    we surprised one day
a proud, tan-spatted, buff-brown pigeon.
    In my hands she flapped so
    fearfully that I let her go.

Her keeper came. And we helped snarl her in a net.
    You bring things I'd as soon forget.

    You raise into my head
a Fall night that I came once more
    to sit on your bed;
sweat beads stood out on your arms and fore-
    head and you wheezed for breath,
    for help, like some child caught beneath
its comfortable woolly blankets, drowning there.
    your lungs caught and would not take the air.

    Of all things, only we
have power to choose that we should die;
    nothing else is free
in this world, to refuse it. Yet I,
    who say this, could not raise
    myself from bed how many days
to the thieving world. Child, I have another wife,
    another child. We try to choose our life.

4.

Here in the scuffled dust
    is our ground of play.
I lift you on your swing and must
    shove you away,
see you return again,
    drive you off again, then

stand quiet till you come.
    You, though you climb
higher, farther from me, longer,
    will fall back to me stronger.
Bad penny, pendulum,
    you keep my constant time

to bob in blue July
    where fat goldfinches fly
over the glittering, fecund
    reach of our growing lands.
Once more now, this second,
    I hold you in my hands.

5.

I thumped on you the best I could
    which was no use;
you would not tolerate your food
until the sweet, fresh milk was soured
    with lemon juice.

That puffed you up like a fine yeast.
    The first June in your yard
like some squat Nero at a feast
you sat and chewed on white, sweet clover.
    That is over.

When you were old enough to walk
    we went to feed
the rabbits in the park milkweed;
saw the paired monkeys, under lock,
    consume each other's salt.

Going home we watched the slow
stars follow us down Heaven's vault.
You said, let's catch one that comes low,
    pull off its skin
and cook it for our dinner.

    As absentee bread-winner,
I seldom got you such cuisine;
we ate in local restaurants
or bought what lunches we could pack
    in a brown sack
with stale, dry bread to toss for ducks
    on the sun-scummed lagoons,
crackers for porcupine and fox,
life-savers for the footpad coons
    to scour and rinse,

snatch after in their muddy pail
    and stare into their paws.
When I moved next door to the jail
    I learned to fry

Omelettes and griddlecakes so I

could set you supper at my table.
As I built back from helplessness,
      when I grew able,
the only possible answer was
      you had to come here less.

This Hallowe'en you come one week.
      You masquerade
      as a vermilion, sleek,
fat, crosseyed fox in the parade
or, where grim jackolanterns leer,

go with your bag from door to door
foraging for treats. How queer:
      when you take off your mask
my neighbors must forget and ask
      whose child you are.
Of course you lose your appetite,
      whine and won't touch your plate;
      as local law
I set your place on an orange crate
in your own room for days. At night

you lie asleep there on the bed
      and grate your jaw.
Assuredly your father's crimes
      are visited
on you. You visit me sometimes.
The time's up. Now our pumpkin sees
      me bringing your suitcase.
      He holds his grin;
the forehead shrivels, sinking in.
You break this year's first crust of snow

off the runningboard to eat.
      We manage, though for days
I crave sweets when you leave and know
They rot my teeth. Indeed our sweet
foods leave us cavities.

6.

The vicious winter finally yields
        the green winter wheat;
the farmer, tired in the tired fields
        he dare not leave, will eat.

Once more the runs come fresh; prevailing
        piglets, stout as jugs,
hurry their old sow to the railing
        to ease her swollen dugs
and game colts trail the herded mares
        that circle the pasture courses;
our seasons bring us back once more
        like merry-go-round horses.

With crocus mouths, perennial hungers,
        into the park Spring comes;
we roast hot dogs on old coat hangers
        and feed the swan bread crumbs,

pay our respects to the peacocks, rabbits,
        and leathery Canada goose
who took, last Fall, our tame white habits
        and now will not turn loose.

In full regalia, the pheasant cocks
        march past their dubious hens;
the porcupine and the lean, red fox
        trot around bachelor pens

and the miniature painted train
        wails on its oval track;
you said, I'm going to Pennsylvania!
        and waved. And you've come back.

If I loved you, they said, I'd leave
        and find my own affairs.
Well, once again this April, we've
        come around to the bears;

punished and cared for, behind bars,

the coons on bread and water
stretch thin black fingers after ours.
And you are still my daughter.

April Inventory

The green catalpa tree has turned
All white; the cherry blooms once more.
In one whole year I haven't learned
A blessed thing they pay you for.
The blossoms snow down in my hair;
The trees and I will soon be bare.

The trees have more than I to spare.
The sleek, expensive girls I teach,
Younger and pinker every year,
Bloom gradually out of reach.
The pear tree lets its petals drop
Like dandruff on a tabletop.

The girls have grown so young by now
I have to nudge myself to stare.
This year they smile and mind me how
My teeth are falling with my hair.
In thirty years I may not get
Younger, shrewder, or out of debt.

The tenth time. Just a year ago,
I made myself a little list
Of all the things I'd ought to know;
Then told my parents, analyst,
And everyone who's trusted me
I'd be substantial, presently.

I haven't read one book about
A book or memorized one plot.
Or found a mind I didn't doubt.
I learned one date. And then forgot.
And one by one the solid scholars
Get the degrees, the jobs, the dollars.

And smile above their starchy collars.

I taught my classes Whitehead's notions;
One lovely girl, a song of Mahler's.
Lacking a source-book or promotions,
I showed one child the colors of
A luna moth and how to love.

I taught myself to name my name,
To bark back, loosen love and crying;
To ease my woman so she came,
To ease an old man who was dying.
I have not learned how often I
Can win, can love, but choose to die.

I have not learned there is a lie
Love shall be blonder, slimmer, younger;
That my equivocating eye
Loves only by my body's hunger;
That I have poems, true to feel,
Or that the lovely world is real.

While scholars speak authority
And wear their ulcers on their sleeves
My eyes in spectacles shall see
These trees procure and spend their leaves.
There is a value underneath
The gold and silver in my teeth.

Though trees turn bare and girls turn wives,
We shall afford our costly seasons;
There is a gentleness survives
That will outspeak and has its reasons.
There is a loveliness exists,
Preserves us. Not for specialists.

The Marsh

Swamp strife and spatterdock
      lull in the heavy waters;
some thirty little frogs
      spring with each step you walk;
a fish's belly glitters
      tangled by rotting logs.

Over near the grey rocks
        muskrats dip and circle.
Out of his rim of ooze
        a silt-black pond snail walks
inverted on the surface
toward what food he may choose.

You look up; while you walk
        the sun bobs and is snarled
in the enclosing weir
        of trees, in their dead stalks.
Stick in the mud, old heart,
what are you doing here?

DAVE ST. CLAIR

How Many Reasons

Along each line dropping off time
Take a page and rearrange the words
Allow it to happen
Then reinvented more of me than
The thoughts allow
Perhaps something is missing
Building as I go along
Philosophy and historical revelation
A new beginning, a story learnt
As a boy. The whole Bible
Beneath which states
I drag a stick along the beach
And watch as the tide comes
And takes my heart away
There in La Conner Washington
Resurrecting the memory
An idea passing through
Fragments little bits
Here and there
Stopping as I go along
A path, a journey
Where souls have a way
Of doing things differently
From what we do here
In this world.

Closing the Shop

It might take years
of waiting. We used to open
at regular hours
we had a plan, a proper investment
a property that paid for itself,
and of course we sold things
over the counter.

We were Marxists then
believers in

the very last thing possible
a revolution in the mode of production
a change in the world order
a philosophy based on the ideas
of some old master
someone beyond the area
of the universities

forced to leave we had dreams
to realize
it took me years even decades
to get this far.
what has become of me
now I have no ideologies
thinking of heroin
and if I were to return to my old days
homeless and on the road
I still wouldn't be able to marry
And make a better life for me.

Dear Barry

I hope you are having a very nice
holiday, oh when the new year blooms.
When the need to compose,
of course, it is as addictive
as food, the absolutes being
an absence of conceptual thought
switch off the forms.
Go beyond, this coming year
starts quite soon. The logic
of calendar days, the usual notions
how the mind works
and how exactly does it work
if I had to work as a secretary
I presume I would lose my touch
and never again produce anything
creative.

Now as I draw to a close, meaning of
course, that I have run out of words

when of course, maltezers
and rocket ships. Harry, he was
a chap I once knew. He said
"got no time for dialogue"
we hardly passed a sentence,
I was the alphabet and he the theme
he became someone, or whom.
Then as I blurr out the last paragraph
and does that mean anything
I hold up the dictionary then slam
that was when I stopped writing.

The Return of the Future

This novel is my first attempt.
up again, looking at men. AS I stared thru
the prison bars, my first, for nine days.
Men showering, fellow prisoners,
Normally I wouldn't, but their humanity,
rather like swimming naked,
and seeing a blonde hair man
covering his genitals with his
guitar, and looking at me, in reply,
then I turned away.
And dived into the water, barely missing
my head on a rock. So he said.
"Be careful, next time."
I don't remember my reply, I do
though recall climbing up the hill,
and driving away with Margot Tyler.
She was as he was, a member of the same band
they came to the Truckee river rising
festival, where I met both of them.
And fell in love with Reno.
No. Miss Tyler from N.Y.
she lived in a cabin up Alleghany
ridge, where else but his territory.

The Philosophies

Take Plato for instance
concretions and formations
idealities organizations
Doreen
Leslie Joseph
strokened tribalities
Kim Guyana
Jackie ex husband
edification beagles
winoutings
a desk of words, chalk marks
and inglish fishing
thru my sky full of
cumulus nimbus clouds
that is what I thought I saw
when at the early age of eleven
I can't squeeze much more out
I stop stop stop...
'It' from moving
every time I wrote it down
black white water ever there is
the typewriter its colours and shapes
and wonder what it is I am using it for
Does writing matter does it matter if
I move my mind out of the equation
Even acting out a role.

Big Brother Watching

Hallucinations, delusions, voices.
figuratively speaking, a Kafka.

Part and parcel, drawn like a moth
in need of the light
the shadows around the objects
their colours and sizes
how in fact they were made
the material labour
the man working for wages
which he can spend

in the supermarkets
the car running on gasoline
the prices rising
climbing to the top
where money is the sole purpose
even as property and mortgages
rise,
the time, one sacrifices
for the basics
where is the freedom in that
where is the truth
what is a person,, if he refuses
to sell what he does
when words are tools, we all share
that is if we can read or write
pop idols, actors, etc
charismatic leadership, the politicians
the bill gates of this world
Change, changing reality, porche, Virginia city.

The New Thing

Towards a place
I burnt the Magic Doctrine
torn in two
I left school
I cruised downtown
after a football match
hooting and hollering
as Reno bet Wooster

then up keystone to the Shakeys
pizza parlour.

I have regretted so much
things did happen then
like the time I slept with Vim
denial doesn't get one anyway
being reborn following Christ
or whoever is in fashion
the truth is I don't know
and within the garden

I was watching Adam and Eve
I don't see why they felt so ashamed
I mean, even If I followed the hippy dream
I was unable then as now to find
the only thing worth listening to
was the sound and content of my mind
I am speaking to myself, pausing as I go
defining what I know as personal
experience.

GEOFF STEVENS

Phalanger

Close your ranks
survival is in the hands
of falangists

positive ideas
marching in unison

pushing away opposition
with their pointed spears

protecting themselves
with a phalanx of shields

finger bones working together
to take a grip on things

their toes pushing themselves forwards
and slowly driving the enemy
into the back of their minds

thus freeing themselves from obsessive occupation

Pelota

Antagonised by demons
you push them away

but the more you drive them off
the more they come back at you

dismiss them
and they return with a fury

belt them out of sight
and they strike back with increased venom

This game you have got yourself into
is a type of isotonic tennis

which uses your own strength
to destroy you
Reverberating from the walls of your mind
it targets you

but cease fighting back
and the demons also will cease

Point of Departure

Men, in black overcoats and brimmed hats,
stand on the bare cobbled quayside,
as the sea begins to glow with the sun's
daily incendary raid,
their backs to the funeral,
the burying of the city in bombs.
It's buildings stand like sledge-hammered tombstones
in a graveyard oversown with unwanted attention.
No boats can take these people back from where they came.

Hyena

Dogs howled death

in the damp, grey air,
the atmosphere as dry as bones

and anticipation stuck in the throat
of a future full of certainty.

I was a child.

What would I have to swallow
when the time came?

At the street end,
with its drizzled line of houses

was the epicentre
of the earthquake

the thump thump thump
from behind the grimed

brick walls that would open
and let me in at 14 years of age.

From the fall of the corrugated
iron roofs, of foundry,

came change. The dogs are in power,
but they still howl

and their propaganda
thumps down on hallway floors.

The foundry was a scare,
but a holiday compared

to today's not knowing
but suspecting

that The Party's power press
is mass-producing

lies.
And all is in reality a lot worse.....

Pneumonicosis

Pneumonicosis,
lungs black and solidified
with foundry sand

and yet my Father
was brilliant at inflating balloons
and at blow-football.

I used to wish
that I could spit as proficiently
as he did -

a fast, direct,
and accurate ball of spittle,
not a misguided dribble.

When the phlegm
moved on his chest,
he'd spit it out

into the fireplace coals,
where the flickering blue flames
of sulphur burnt,

and it would sizzle there,
like the anger of snake venom,
until it boiled away.

In the City at Night

In the city at night
the cars move slowly
and driverless
pedestrians are dark silhouettes
against a black background
and buildings dissolve
leaving only their lighted windows
their button-badge neon identities
and their hardness
when one walks into them.
Below a streetlamp
lit by their foreheads
their noses, their cheekbones,
people pass the time wailing
for a bus
by pulling grotesque faces.

RICHARD STEWART

Hares at Fakenham Wood

There is a majesty about hares
Difficult to define or decipher,
Well beyond the urbane
Usage of similes or metaphors.
A roe deer, rippling like raw silk
Through a field of barley,
Runs it close

But a hare seems to move
As if having shed all conscious effort
No longer of simple substance
But existing in another dimension.

And Boudicca marching to Camulodunum.
The blood lust strong in her breast,
Knew it too, let one pass
Unmolested through her war camp
On the eve of battle, thankful
that the Gods had sent
Such a messenger to bless their cause.

BENITO STOAKES

My Father's Song

Hope

has grown from
whispers, a new baby is born;
this, I refer to, was yesterday a long
maybe seventeen years. A winding since
has passed me by, angled with tears.
    But these sharp angles move, like
bitter tastes sweetening, in and above my blue eyes
(my soul as island) to it in waves:
    another life, aspiring.

Before the sea tolls its last
    and carcasses wait

other lives, to mine, those mysterious tires
burn on
to your wide shoulders and frailty:
myself in new acres,
o son!

ELIZABETH TANSLEY

The Ward

She effortlessly lights a cigarette puffing away like a steam
                                        engine
Oblivious to the others watching television absorbing daytime
                                        TV
A woman hesitates then goes over to the one with the keys
The nurse shakes her head - tedium has set in like dry rot
Arguments flare up .. .the nurse leaves.

Patients huddled in groups waiting for visitors smoking away
                                    minutes
That become hours discussing symptoms
Music plays like a backdrop in comes the nurse to observe
'Would you like to go to OT?' some leave
heads bowed like children ushered into a classroom I decline.

Subjects on offer- drawing, painting plates, making cards
Useless activities for ornaments and cards you don't want
Courses on computers that I've already done
A library with old books of historical romance
Days become weeks...

Quizzes I don't mind - then I am allowed out in the hospital
                                     grounds
Problem is I've only two pounds to last me
An hour a day
Nights spent pill popping
Watching TV.

Two weeks later I'm allowed to the shops
Two hours a day
On the ward patients wait for psychiatrists who appear hours
                                        later
Those on leave wait for pills that should be ready at 1pm arrive
                                        at 8pm
The ward is merely a waiting room nurses sit in the staff room
                              for hours on end
Chattering...

Self harmers receive immediate attention whilst the quiet ones
                                            are ignored
Nurses have their favourites
I get day leave and retreat to my flat glad of familiar things.
Now I am an adult away from the ward that treats like children
Dispensing pills like treats for good behaviour.
A month later I am discharged nothing changes in all my visits
                                            to the ward

BARRY TEBB

Reflecting on Wordsworth

I wandered through the streets of Leeds
As lonely as I always am, a Saturday
Of cold March wind when suddenly a storm began
And flurries through the stalls were sent
As frenziedly the market men rushed off to pack
But not before I'd snatched 'The Clanceys Best'
And stowed it lovingly away between Lacan
And my first novel, arrived from heat and dust
Of Kolkatta to be corrected in red ink, redundant words
To be excised and then I travelled to the ward.
The faience tiles of domed arcades deep in the jubilation
Of their spring and deep within a muted voice had whispered 'Sing.'

But could a singer find a song on that clear day?
Among the blanked out faces on the ward
Sad eyes in disarray were watching me
So I went on to find without a warmer air
The rain had washed and stars had spun
Their traceries within my mind's enclave
Where shades of muses raised wan faces
In supermarket queues. Ali, Jean and Chris
My thoughts return to you, O lovely triad
I so miss, one dead, one lost, one found and lost again
Without a parting kiss so I pressed on to find
The college in my mind, a Rubicon I could not cross
Where halls of residence had multiplied and asked
Why no one had remarked the absence of the three
Since term began and pleaded for a scan of lists
But sudden gusts blew all away and in such loneliness
I had to cry for muses gone beyond the ken
Of mortal man and I was left to wander
And to weep in all the muted turbulence of sleep.

To the Sound of Violins

Give me life at its most garish
Friday night in the Square, pink sequins dazzle
And dance on clubbers bare to the midriff

Young men in crisp shirts and pressed pants
'Dress code smart' gyrate to 'Sex Bomb, Sex Bomb'
And sing along its lyrics to the throng of which I'm one
My shorts, shoulder bag and white beard
Making me stand out in the teeming swarm
Of teens and twenties this foetid Friday night
On my way from the ward where our son paces
And fulminates I throw myself into the drowning
Tide of Friday to be rescued by sheer normality.

The mill girl with her mates asks anxiously
"Are you on your own? Come and join us
What's your name?" Age has driven my shyness away
As I join the crowd beneath the turning purple screens
Bannered 'Orgasm lasts for ever' and sip unending
Halves of bitter, as I circulate among the crowd,
Being complete in itself and out for a good night out,
A relief from factory, shop floor and market stall
Running from the reality of the ward where my son
Pounds the ledge with his fist and seems out to blast
My very existence with words like bullets.

The need to anaesthetise the pain resurfaces
Again and again. In Leeds City Square where
Pugin's church, the Black Prince and the Central Post Office
In its Edwardian grandeur are startled by the arching spumes
Or white water fountains and the steel barricades of Novotel
Rise from the ruins of a sixties office block.
I hurry past and join Boar Lane's Friday crew
From Keighley and Dewsbury's mills, hesitating
At the thought of being told I'm past my
Sell-by-date and turned away by the West Indian
Bouncers, black-suited and city-council badged
Who checked my bag but smiled at 'The Lights of
Leeds' and 'Poets of Our Time' tucked away
      as carefully as condoms-
Was it guns or drugs they were after
I wondered as I crossed the bare boards to the bar.
I stayed near the fruit machine which no-one played,
Where the crowd was thickest, the noise drowned out the pain
'Sex Bomb, Sex Bomb' the chorus rang
The girls joined in but the young men knew

The words no more than me. Dancing as we knew it
In the sixties has gone, you do your own thing
And follow the beat, hampered by my bag
I just kept going, letting the music and the crowd
Hold me, my camera eye moving in search, in search...

What I'm searching for I don't know
Searching's a way of life that has to grow
"All of us who are patients here are searchers after truth"
My son kept saying, his legs shaking from the side effects
Of God-knows- what, pacing the tiny ward kitchen cum smoking room,
Denouncing his 'illegal section' and 'poisonous medication'
To an audience of one.
The prospect of TV, Seroxat and Diazepan fazed me:
I was beyond unravelling Meltzer on differentiation
Of self and object or Rosine Josef Perelberg on
      'Dreaming and Thinking'
Or even the simpler 'Rise and Crisis of Psychoanalysis
      in the United States'
So I went out with West Yorkshire on a Friday night.

Nothing dramatic happened; perhaps I'm a little too used
To acute wards or worse where chairs fly across rooms,
Windows disintegrate and double doors are triple locked
And every nurse carries a white panic button and black pager
To pinpoint the moment's crisis. Normality was
      a bit of adrenaline,
A wild therapy that drew me in, sanity had won the night.
"Are you on your own, love? Come and join us"
People kept asking if I was alright and why
I had that damned great shoulder bag. I was introduced
To three young men about to tie the knot, a handsome lothario
In his midforties winked at me constantly,
Dancing with practised ease with sixteen year olds
Who all seemed to know him and determined to show him.

Three hours passed in as many minutes and then the crowds
Disappeared to catch the last bus home. The young aren't
As black as they are painted, one I danced with reminded me
Of how Margaret would have been at sixteen
With straw gold hair Yeats would have immortalised.
People seemed to guess I was haunted by an inner demon

I'd tried to leave in the raftered lofts of City Square
But failed to. Girls from sixteen to twenty six kept grabbing me
And making me dance and I found my teenage inhibitions
Gone at sixty-one and wildly gyrated to
      'Sex Bomb, Sex Bomb'
Egged on by the throng by the fruit machine and continuous
Thumbs-up signs from passing men. I had to forgo
A cheerful group of Aussies were intent on taking me clubbing
"I'd get killed or turned into a pumpkin
If I get home after midnight" I quipped to their delight
But being there had somehow put things right.

Infamous Poet

I never did fit in – at six or sixty one –
I stand out in a crowd, too young or old
And gather pity like a shroud. "Is that real silk?"
A teenager inquired. "As real as Oxfam ever is
For one pound fifty." The vast ballroom was growing misty
And blurred with alcohol I've never had the taste for.
"Fuck off" a forty-plus dyed blonde said half in jest.
So I chose the only Asian girl in Squares with hair like jet
And danced with her five minutes centre stage –
I've lost all inhibitions in old age. A Malaysian architecture
Student invited me to sit and get my breath back
"Le Corbusier described a house as a machine for living in,"
I quipped; she slipped a smile and sipped her drink and said
"I love Leeds and its people; in seven years I've never
Heard a single racist comment, whatever the papers say"
Malaysian girls are rightly known for their sensual beauty
But I made my pitiful excuses and slipped away.
I knew I couldn't make it, couldn't even fake it
With all this damned depression in the way.

Leeds boys are always friendlier than the girls,
They see themselves grown older in my years
And push the girls towards me with a glance
"Go and give the poor old man a dance!"
And dance I do and show my poems around
Like calling cards and jot lines on my palms.
Reading Lacan into the night I thought things through
But somehow none of them was half as good as you.

To the Memory of My Mother

This is one spring you will not see.
The fifty roses of your spray
Smelt soft across that February day
Where trees, heavy as only crematoria
Can bear, sloped down the fallen banks
To where we waited in the chapel, me
Clutching Father Kevin's hand, remembering
My given grace and faith renewed
In answer to my prayers, Brenda in tears,
And Joyce the sister of my years, Kim
And the others from the Home, where five
Long years you waited for this day,
Of all, the most important. Visits, letters,
Phone calls far too few, until we knew
When your last days began and for sixteen
Hours we sat, but still your will to live
Went on until our backs were turned
And then you, too, had gone.

A Fine Madness

Any poets about or bored muses fancying a day out?
Rainy, windy, cold Leeds City Station
Half-way through its slow chaotic transformation
Contractors' morning break, overalls, hard hats and harness
Flood McDonalds where I sip my tea and try
      to translate Valéry.

London has everything except my bardic inspiration
I've only to step off the coach in Leeds and it whistles
Its bravuras down every wind, rattles the cobbles in Kirkgate Market
Hovers in the drunken brogue of a Dubliner in the chippie
As we share our love of Joyce the Aire becomes the Liffey.

All my three muses have abandoned me. Daisy in Asia,
Brenda protesting outside the Royal Free, Barbara seeing clients at the
C.A.B.
Past Saltaire's Mill, the world's eighth wonder,
The new electric train whisperglides on wet rails
Past Shipley's fairy glen and other tourist trails

Past Kirkstall's abandoned abbey and redundant forge
To Grandma Wild's in Keighley where I sit and gorge.

I've travelled on the Haworth bus so often
The driver chats as if I were a local
But when the rainbow's lightning flash
Illumines all the valleys there's a hush
And every pensioner's rheumy eye is rooted
On the gleaming horizon as its mooted
The Bronte's spirits make the thunder crack
Three cloaked figures converging round the Oakworth track.

Haworth in a storm is a storm indeed
The lashing and the crashing makes the gravestones bleed
The mashing and the bashing makes the light recede
And on the moor top I lose my way and find it
Half a dozen times slipping in the mud and heather
Heather than can stand the thrust of any weather.
Just as suddenly as it had come the storm abated
Extremes demand those verbs so antiquated
Archaic and abhorred and second-rated
Yet still they stand like moorland rocks in mist
And wait as I do till the storm has passed
Buy postcards at the parsonage museum shop
Sit half an hour in the tea room drying off
And pen a word or two to my three muses
Who after all presented their excuses
But nonetheless the three all have their uses.

To Daisy Abey

In sleep I dream the gratitude I know I cannot say
Now you are in latitude where palm trees hold the sway
There are always things between us
    that keep getting in the way
And stop me from expressing the things I mean to say
In a night of wind and weathers love will not go away.

Winterlight

Let us, this December night, leave the ring
Of heat, the lapping flames around the fire's heart,
Move with bodies tensed against the light
Towards the moon's pull and the cloud's hand.
Arms of angels hold us, lend our bodies
Height of stars and the planets' whirl,
Grant us sufficiency of light so we may enter
The twisting lanes to lost villages.

So we may stare in the mirror of silent pools
By long-deserted greens, deepen our sight
Of what lies beyond the things that seem
And make our vision clear as winterlight.

Paris

Stretching out beyond the *banlieus*
Of barricades and burnt-out cars.
Les Halles a jungle of weeds
And rust where Zola's ghost shuffles
Along abandoned galleries
Scribbling ferociously he notes the lives of the homeless
For his next *opus*, among the chick weed
And the broken stones.

Mozart at the Trianion, Mass at Sacré Coeur
Where the Montmontre Express, a toy train
Trundles over cobbles, among the stalls
Where scarlet saris thread the February morning
The cobbles accommodate MacDonalds
Opposite Bedouin wares, woven gold blouses
And Joponaiserai.

A girl in the metro is intent
On Baudelaire, their last Bohemian;
George Barker was ours, thirteen or was it
Fifteen children on the farm at Ittertingham
From his several wives.

This Used to be a Day Hospital

The Community Team's lease had run out,
The rent was to be upped so they shut up shop
And the team re-opened in a unit closed
Two years ago – the sign still said in rusting red
Chiltern Day Hospital and the empty frames
Of windows blew in the February wind, grass
Had grown between paving stones and the contractors
Were busy ripping out the day hospital signs.
Dining room, art therapy, patients lounge,
So much rubbish to be binned, the view of trees
The patients drew for decades was the only item
Not for the chop and as I sat in the makeshift
Waiting room the wind whistled,
The corrugated roof was a drum and I heard it beat
The last retreat in the sombre pearl grey morning
When I knew the light had gone
From those who came daily to meet friends,
To be looked after and most of all be kept alive.

A sudden decision made closure inevitable
There is no longer a hospital, no more day care
The ghosts of the patients have nowhere.

The Road to Haworth Moor
for Brenda Williams

The dawn cracked with ice, with fire grumbling in the grate,
With ire in the homes we had left, but still somehow
We made a nook in the crooked corner of Hall Ings,
A Wordsworthian dream with sheep nibbling by
      every crumbling
Dry-stone wall, smoke inching from the chimney pot beside the
Turning lane, the packhorse road with every stone
      intact that bound
The corner tight then up and off to Thurstonland,
      past the weathered
Walls of the abandoned quarry, beyond Ings Farm where
      Rover ran
His furious challenge to our call.

We had little, so little it might have been nothing at all
The few hundred books we'd brought and furniture bought
At auction in the town, left-overs knocked down
      to the few pounds
We had between us, dumped outside the red front door by the
Carrier's cart; stared at by neighbours constantly grimacing
Though the grimy nets of the weavers' cottage windows,   baffled
As to who we were and how and why we'd come there.

I never gave it a thought (perhaps I should have) but with
The sense of 'poet' in my soul, a book to read and one
To write, night walks in the valley's hyaline air through
Brambled woods and on down tracks we trekked along
Until the sharp sneck of dawn drew us back to the
One-up one-down cottage on the lumbering hill.

Was it folly, chance or madness, another's or our own,
Drove us from Leeds, our native home, past shadows
Darker than death itself upon the bedroom wall
At Rawdon in the bungalow by the cross-roads where we met?
Three decades on and yet I cannot say for sure the destiny
That made us meet was dark or light, some sound or sight
'Beyond our mortal vision', some immaterial infinity,
A double helix on the heels of both that made my south
Your north and jerked the compass till we knew
Not day from night nor wrong from right.

Only a week ago you took me to the house you came from
Thirty years before. Together we stood as strangers in a room
Filled with plastic saccharine furniture, vinyl gloss, cabinets
Of china dogs and photographs of a departed wife and child.
All that remained of your family was a hidden coat of red paint
Beneath the kitchen windowsill and on a faded page
      the number for
Your long-gone neighbour, Lilly Clarke,
      ninety if she lives at all,
The memory of a lilac tree, the Anderson shelter
      hidden by the fence,
And the incomer's invitation to call again and then and then...

We were wrong from the beginning, you always said, wrong
To be together, wrong to go away or perhaps,

                as Hobsbaum said,
'It was the place's fault. If we'd made it to Haworth as we
Dreamed, standing on the moor top, the heather
                muffling your tears,
The wind sighing its threnody, crying its cradle-song, whispering
Promises of its care to come, its breath caressing
                the very stones
We sat on, lost beyond the ken of any guide,
                beyond the signatures
Of time and place, beyond, beyond...

2.

There is no clock can measure what we both passed through,
The darker griefs that soon began to haunt your fragile sleep,
The echoes of nightmare flights through
                empty streets that soon
Began to creep behind the wainscot of those tiny rooms, the rat
That took them up and ran to hide and haunt us, encountered
At the cellar-head or heard beneath the boards.
                The sad rat-catcher's
Nod and shaking head, as if he knew more than the pair of us
What lay ahead. Like Charlotte's your hair lay in dark ringlets
On the pillow while I lay stunned and terrified and lost.
From then till now, two children grew, two fathers died;
One mad, one sad, but both alone. Together or apart our lives
Have changed beyond repair, the text altered and the cover bare
But still the same story more or less, echoing
                down hospital corridors,
Left in faded waiting rooms and lost/ like our children,

Cyril Williams, gravedigger at Killingbeck, buried among
The graves his own hands dug, lay beside your mother,
'In death as in life together,' - what parody lies hidden
Beneath the marble chips of the unmarked grave?
Where is the cross of weathered wood and stapled names?
The thirty roses that you left had withered on the stem,
The weeds had spread and spread and you yourself
Were paler than the dead.

There may be little time or time enough for ills
We have to bear for others with our own. Madness

Seems our calling, yours and mine, speaking a tongue
Where words are symbols, signs and symptoms, pointers
To a buried past, clues to an untold murder.
Those nightmares came to haunt us and teach us and take us
To that room in Stainmore Place, your mother's ghost
At Banquo's feast, the guest that never could
Be laid to rest.

3.

One stifling July day thirty years on we returned to Honley
Where the hamlet snagged on the hillside,
       fattened now and hollow
And grown grey with money and success:
       one cottage joined on
To the next, the common land fenced off, the nearby chapel
Turned to a desirable residence, the tombstones
       garden ornaments,
The heart of Hall Ings Mill crumpled under
       mechanical hammers
And reeled before our eyes, dust rising to powder the wings
Of passing butterflies. We watched the white-glazed
       inner walls
Sink in shame to shattered heaps of stone and
       shards of nothingness.

I never thought it would be the experience it was—
How could anything be more banal than a visit to Oakes?
Twenty two Georgian semis from the sixties,
       brass coach-lamps
By glass front doors, irreproachable gardens,
The estate lodge's great oak doors opening to vistas
Of street on street, the fields and cattle gone.
We peered through the polished windows at the hearth
We'd sat around, our hearts numb, but then
A quiet came we had not felt for years, a lens of silence
Enclosed us, a single leaf fell at my feet.

4.

The rat we tried to frighten, trap or poison, saw us off instead;
It seemed as if it grew beneath our very skins and circled

With our blood and hammered at our heads and
    leered from specks
Of fluff beneath the bed. The wainscot was the worst,
    it seemed
No whitewashed wall was free from cavities that wound behind
And joined another maze of runs that opened to the
    boards of yet
Another floor, until the tiny house had grown to
    one great rat-run
Vaster than the universe, where that single rodent
    gnawed and slithered
To unsettle finally our fragile peace.

I did not want to go. You did. I could not stay alone. It was
The whispers said and never ceased, 'the beginning of the end'.
Now, thirty odd years on, I do not know at all,
    no certainty is certain,
No narrative, however neat, is sure. I know how listlessly
    we tried
Again in Leeds, a tiny flat with the white telephone that
    never rang
Next to the Christian Science Church my sad grandmother
    trekked to with
Her cancer-ridden spine. It was doomed from the start.
    The previous
Tenants had ended in divorce. If the certain salesman and
    his gleaming
Bride had failed to make it, how could we? Our moves
    from Huddersfield

And back became more frantic and our peace more fragile.
You always felt lonely in the countryside,
    while in Leeds I longed
For open vistas cloud-masses over the blue chain of hills,
    the silence
Of the lanes, the sheep bells and the endless walks.
    Was I in flight..?
You had to ask but then as now I had no answer;
    but it's the way I was,
Hating the clutter of the city, man en masse.
    I thought I needed a mate

For a Platonic cave, a companion for the Martello tower
> in Dublin Bay,
Whatever it was I never wanted you to go
> but go you did to stay.
The one became the two again, you shed your ring,
> we had our son to share.
I read instead of writing, psycho-analysis became
> a faith of sorts,
A pastime then a passion I kept on with even when
> my muse returned
Demanding me in dreams. Our children grew,
> then you wrote, too, by candle
In the dark or by the breath of the midnight sea
> on Brighton beach.
You made the rat return so I could face it, retracing childhood's
Nightmare footsteps while you recalled the terror of countless
Nights and days until I understood the meaning of
> our parted ways.

5.

If only we could go back to the cottage on the hill at Honley
Where the road sweeps gently under the bridge
> where trains never ran
Our voices still echoing round the cavernous walls
> the smooth moss clings to
And we are beyond the reach of the driving rain.

There is always the odd cottage no one can be bothered with   where the
lorries roar
But when you look behind a random stream gurgles by
> an overgrown track
With a gully of pebbles and overhanging rock,
The door still hangs on that rusty latch; your thumb might still
Make it yield, not in the *sturm und drang* of adolescence but in
The quieter intimacies of shared grief.

The hills have not moved nor the clouds altered the
> stance of their lazy azure
Nor has the watery Pennine sun gone in before
> the swallows gather.

Perhaps I have lost that *jouissance*-and who would
    not given the tornadoes,
Undivined and undeserved that seized our lives in
    their burning fury,
Leaving us awake in a world of dark horizons and
    troubled days,
Our memory a cave of broken shards.

One death came when a brother and a mother gathered
    so that a father
Might die opportunely and without succour in
    a hill-top hospital,
Lonely as a scarecrow and inaccessible on the
    moorland midnight,
Beyond the reach of all but death standing at the bed-head.

Similarly your own father blundering
    'into the Selby Road, high on morphine'
Could only end in the same way.

These griefs were only too normal, as was
    my mother's death you wrote of
With such sad eloquence as you shared my vigil:
    nothing could be added
To your lines.

And of it all and of what I cannot speak?
The silence in Gethsemane
The breaking of bread
The communion when the wine I drank
Made your cradle Catholic soul
Fret at my insouciance.

6.

Waking early I felt my sixty years
The winters of childhood slipping and sliding
In my tired imagination, the icicles on the kitchen window,
The ashes scattered over paths in patches of grey and black.

We have so much to comprehend, too much for any mortal,
The madness of youth, so fierce, so compulsive,

The cocktails of alcohol and drugs, the quarrels
    with knives and guns
Entered into as lightly as love was once with us.

Our generation awaits the taste of death
With none of the anticipated solace,
No children's children visiting in spite of the spare room
Stacked with toys, with shelves of dusty books, Baum's 'Magical Land of Oz'
Its spine laid bare, Mombi the witch, Dorothy and Toto
Gathered forlornly round the saw-horse,
    the scarlet and crimson
Of their Edwardian rig slightly ridiculous, the Gothic typeface
Evoking sepia prints of my father at five in a pinafore or seven
In a sailor-suit feeding the Sunday birds, my grandmother
Framed in a trellis of *mignonette,* the aroma fragrant still,
The violet stock lingering and re-kindling our first garden
The autumn we moved in, the rampant blossoms cager
    in the soil
Of my father's first sowing.

For us there was no garden, the cottage at Hall lngs
Had only a paved yard, with tufts of grass and lichen
The whole country round an abundance of hedges and ditches
Where dog-roses blossomed, meadows of cow-parsley,
    stiles to field paths,
The weathered sign 'To Thurstonland' we followed with
    hand-in-hand innocence,
Returning at sunset, our hands full of violets.

The garden at Oakes stayed barren, thc bare soil
    cumbered with builder's waste,
Resisting our listless endeavours. The jobbing
    gardener stirred Paraquat,
Muttering under his breath as he sheltered
    in the garage from the sudden rain.
He left the seeding to another day,
    left it too late to sow, grumbled
As he turfed it the day after our move with Brenda alone,
Scrubbing the boards. She saw him scowl
    as he punched the limp turf
With his calloused hands, demanding payment,

    angry at her innocence.
Brudenell Road had no garden to speak of,
A couple of feet at the front with a broken wall
And the back bare and hard from children's play,
The privet was matted with shards of glass,
    worn tennis balls and broken toys,
So tattered I cut it back to the wall,
    I sat on the top step and read,
Watching the children play in the sand
    I'd trundled in barrow loads
From the builder's yard, a make-do sandpit which
    drew the whole street,
West Indian, English and Asian built temples together.
    Our sandalled
Bearded neighbour was the first to complain,
    his teacher wife beside him,
The next-door French widow supporting,
    "So numerous the children, n'est ce pas?"
Meaning "Don't encourage the Pakis,
    there are too many already."
Like thunder the row erupted, a streetful of shouting,
    my voice the loudest,
The yesses had it, the children remained,
    our last real garden.

7.

In Memory of Emily Bronte

Besieged, beaten and bruised
I had proved my oracle lied
There was no peace in poetry and flight.
Yet as I sat and watched the night
Gather in the shallows of heather
I remembered the steep stone streets,
The ginnels of my childhood,
The walls of Roman York.

On this last June day, hidden by a haze of walls,
I found a cottage so overgrown I had to part a mass of green
To touch the door, the window-panes opaque with dirt,
    sills choked with books,

A rusted letter-box, cracked lintel,
        lichened roof-slates caving in,
A 'Sold' board hammered firmly into place.

There was no solace in the parsonage, no solace there at all,
The staff found it odd, my wanting to park my
        heavy bag and trudge
From room to room. The couch Emily died on,
        so shabby and so faded,
Patrick's hat and sticks like stage props,
        Mrs. Gaskell's escritoire
So thoroughly bourgeois, Charlotte's crinoline
        evoking 'Ooh' and 'Aah'.

I sat outside the tourist shop, watching the families pass,
Still reeling from the news of our son's loss,
His life-in-death and death-in-life.

The crowds gone, the shops closed
I browsed over rock and lichen,
O sleeper in the earth
Would that you might listen.

Would that you waken and tell me
Why young girls' beauty no longer moves me?
Their innocent glances as they leap-frog or hand-stand
With such *jouissance* takes hold of me no more.

I watched a troupe of Keighley girls
Pass through a turnstile on their way
To clubs in Leeds last night.

One wore a veil tacked round with sequins
Like scruples on the hem: there is no beauty like that girl's
Who's naked feet touched heaven in their swirls.

Note: I use the word 'scruples' in its old sense i.e. a weight of 20 grains.

From **Mooring Posts**

The mooring posts marked on the South Leeds map
Of 1908 still line the Aire's side, huge, red

With rust, they stand by the Council's Transpennine
Trail opposite the bricked and boarded up Hunslet
Mills with trees growing from its top storey, roofless,
Open to the enormous skies of our childhood.

The Aire Suspension Bridge, always *my* bridge,
Has gone from wartime camouflage grey to
Council green with a traffic island in between
The lanes where lorries roar and silent anglers
Stitched along the shore shelter under the
Giant red, green and yellow umbrellas of Monet.

In the Aire's clear waters salmon dart and
Giant trout are basking in the sun;
There is abundant clay for potters' wheels
With haptic stone for sculptors' hands
And the surrounding water is lapis lazuli and ochre.

The steps to the moorings have been carved
Out of indigenous rock and the bridge itself,
Arch by arch, was made of Hunslet iron and brought
On drays two hundred yards from the foundry where
They forged it and it was laid, cantilever by cantilever
By local men hammering home the bolts
From the Hunslet Nail Works.
They fashioned a toll-gate and a keeper came
And sat in a booth with his pipe and a ledger
To take down comings and goings in the curious
Copper-plate of the Hunslet Board School and
Beneath the bridge sailed dhows and catamarans
And coal barges with captains who smoked short
Stubby pipes in shirt-sleeves and Van Gogh was
There to capture them on canvas after canvas.
Vermeer had exactly the touch and his palette
Was right for the chiaroscuro of the back-to-backs;
He got the particular yellow of the donkey-stoned
Steps and the waxed scarlet rinds of the Edam our
Mothers bought up at the Maypole.

There was a heat haze over Accommodation Road
And in it we saw the oases of Kandinsky
And listened to camels' bells
And tasted the dates of the abundant palms.

The Philosophers

Lavender musk rose from the volume I was reading through,
The college crest impressed in gold, tooled
      gold lettering on the spine.
It was not mine but my son's, jammed in the
      corner of a cardboard box
With dozens more; just one box of a score, stored in a heap
Across my ex-wife's floor, our son gone far,
      as far as Samarkand and Ind
To where his strange imaginings had led,
      to heat and dust, some lust
To know Bengali, to translate Tagore, or just, for all we know,
Stroll round those sordid alleys and bazaars and ask for toddy
If it's still the same and say it in a tongue they know.

The Classics books lay everywhere around the flat,
      so many that my mind
Grew numb. Heavy, dusty dictionaries of Mandarin and Greek,
Crumbling Victorian commentaries where
      every *men* and *de* was weighed
And weighed again, and then, through
      a scholar's gloss on Aristotle,
That single sentence glowed, 'And thus we see nobility of soul
Comes only with the conquering of loss';
      meaning shimmered in that empty space
Where we believed there was no way to resurrect
      two sons we'd watched grow up,
One lost to oriental heat and dust, the other to a fate of wards.
It seemed that rainy April Sunday in the
      musty book-lined rooms
Of Brenda's flat, mourning the death of Beethoven,
      her favourite cat,
Watching Mozart's ginger fur, his plaintive tone
      of loss, whether
Some miscreant albatross was laid across our deck,
      or bound around
The ship, or tangled about whatever destiny we moved towards
Across that frozen sea of dark extremity;
      fatigued as if our barque

Had hardly stirred for all those years of strife, for all the times
We'd set the compass right, sorted through
        those heaped up charts
And with fingers weary and bleary-eyed retraced our course.
The books, a thousand books that lined the walls:
Plato's chariot racing across the empty sky,
Sartre's waiters dancing like angels on the heads of pins,
And Wittgenstein, nodding in his smoke-filled Cambridge den,
Dreaming of a school room in the Austrian hills and walks
In mountain air, wondering why he wasn't there.
We wondered, too, at what, if anything we knew,
        trying to sift some
Single fact that might elicit hope from loss,
        enough to get us through
Another year with other griefs to come, we knew.
        Some, by a little,
Through God's grace or chance or simple will, we might delay.
More likely we would have no say. By words or
        actions who can stay
The rolling balls across the table's baize,
        the click of ball on ball,
The line of bottles in the hall?

We heard the ticking of the Roman -figured clock
My mother made us take when all was lost,
Together until the last breath had flown
Into the blue empyrean with her soul.

Death of a Poet

for Wendy Oliver, who knew him

I am the sick animal you dream you are caring for
In the long avenues of night I cannot find a name
For the sickness except the despair of a poet sensing his veins
Silt up like the delta of a neglected river
        with none of the solace
Sidney Graham felt as he lay by Nessie's side
        with Madron's circling
Wood and its snow blanket of comfort falling as he glided
From this world into the next, finger-painting
        his adieux into the small

Of her back, bidding them be hidden beyond
    the tiny bulk of his poems
To be found by the faithful far from the yawning
    taverns of eager tourists.
Alone with Nessie and her shadows in sleep
    as the wood of Madron
Moved slowly towards that final deep.

BRIDGET TEMPLE-JONES

Peace at last

Wintry sun and grey mist
memories drift in the haze
consciousness comes and goes
the wind breathes for me.
Fragments fall soft as snow,
at one with the spirit
that controls my soul,
at peace with my Maker.
I have no fear and no fight
for I am floating high,
high on a Melleril cloud,
there is no pain or torment
no anguish over my sins
just beautiful, pure paralysis.

Something to Get Out of Bed for

I don't want to die old
In pain and miserable.
I don't want to die young
Despite my ailing mind.
I don't want to whinge and moan
And say that life has been a bitch,
All men are bastards,
And I wish and if only.
'Cos there's more to life than this,
There's always a shred of hope,
A distant memory to cling onto,
And something to get out of bed for.

ARCANGELO TINSLEY

Hospital Blues

Numbed by the radio's
oppressive volume,
blinded by artificial
brain-splitting light,
zombified by largactil,
raped by pitiless eyes,
hassled by requests for tobacco,
deafened by crashing pool balls,
invaded by *concerned* observers
and deadened by moronic monotony
        you wonder
as you sip tasteless tea
and scorch your lungs on cheap tobacco -

will freedom ever come?

JOHN TOWERS

Best Day of Our Lives

        oppressive
        obsessive
        suffocating

My years at school
were like being in borstal
a prison sentence
I didn't deserve.

        haunting
        horrifying
        stinking

That smell: dust, sweat
and boiled cabbage.
The long, dim corridors,
the decaying furniture.

        depressing
        distressing
        traumatic

I was supposedly sent there
to be educated, but I learned
more in the playground
than I did from the lessons.

        repressive
        restricting
        stifling

Like a term in the army
to break the spirit and prepare
the young for the factory,
the pit or the sales floor.

        disturbing
        demoralising
        conditioning

Singing hymns at assembly.
Cheering on the football field.
Fights in the playground.
Fires in the chemistry lab.

    petty
    pathetic
    bureaucratic

Amongst those 980 inmates lurked
the future politicians, judges, reporters;
wife beaters, animal abusers, rapists;
drug pushers, paedophiles, murderers.

    undemocratic
    unsympathetic
    totalitarian

A breeding ground for germs.

Night Terror

Another nightmare,
another night lost.
I have dreamed
of the inevitable:
Armageddon.

I look out of the window
while I wait for the kettle.
Back-lit patterned squares
are cut into the darkness
as the workforce rises.
It is seven-seventeen.

The sound of traffic
on the A6 is reassuring.
The rattle of the trains
is a comforting reminder
that it was only a dream.
This time.

I sip my tea and watch the daylight
increasing over the rooftops,
and the coloured squares
blink out one by one.

They - the workforce - line the streets
and fill the stations, while I sit here,
exhausted, but too afraid
to close my eyes.

DANIEL TUOHY

Wonderful Life

Each wonderful day at the asylum
Forty cups of coffee I drink
And once a week I get to speak
To the warm and genial shrink

Redundant

Why not be redundant
Have a life without meaning?
Till you break into an office
To do a bit of cleaning!

How Love Compels

He battered to bits the bloke
Shattered to bits his spine
For looking in a peculiar way
At his funny valentine!

ALEX WARNER

Lonely

Burningly lonely hours
when light falls slowly, softly
faint shadows twist round narrow corners
disappear into narrowing perspective
a navy blue hue overtakes the view
as eve leads into twilight
earlier, a phantom moon
was groomed against a pale blue
horizon, temperature lowering
as I clapped eyes on
the Jesus flag fluttering from
a church steeple.

A bygone Stalybridge winter
with so few people
no narrow boats silently sailing
across canal.
Only a fluttering of wings
as a Canadian goose leans
and follows after its pal.
Icy waters, bland-grey skies.

Ghost town, down-town,
just checking how the land lies.
Most shops shut
Only pubs open.

Few buses to be caught,
Days remain so short,
I will be lonely tonight.
Shadows for company,
Only the moon, for light.

JULIE WHITBY

The Violet Room

The violet room, they called it,
yet we knew otherwise.

Misty, violet curtains hung there:
moistly welcoming, oh yes.

But through their careful lies
we sensed its sumptuous secrets,

judged them dear as wild strawberries,
lay in wait for lurid hints:

an uncut novel in French-
scrumptiously virginal-

and smelling superb to us
as croissants and coffee.

The aroma of tobacco,
not Papa's surely?

A drawer crackling with lace petticoats,
unworn. Why? What for?

Our days had a point, a purpose:
we waited, bided our time.

But nothing decisive
was ever discovered.

We consoled ourselves finally
with Enid Blyton, Jane Austen. Or, unabashed,

tried on Mamma's lipstick
in the dusty mirror of that ghosted room.

At other times wept copiously,
without knowing why, hollow as our dolls.

The violet room we call it now,
Yet they know otherwise.

BRENDA WILLIAMS

Oxford from a Prison Cell

what road did I come by
poetry leads to a locked door and at the last deserts
the body it has used you come to me at the threshold
after seven days and you come as a faithless woman
though the sun coloured iris hurts it breaks towards sunlight
Caltha palustris unearthed closes only to the dark
the body will fight to the death for its own dignity
while the mind more able to imagine a walled up tomb
than a room with a locked door the eternity of one
and the time of the other where the mind free wheeling can
recall only the absurd I sat once with my back to
another door learning Greek for the first time and the last
time learning Greek then you came with cups of kings you
                                        cannot
help me now let's go on together turn and turn about
I will make the songs and you shall grind them out

July 1985

Limen
walk close to the wall the wind will not blow cold there

I could not sit in the tradesmans entrance that was not what
I was there for I see again open carved scrolls open
on the locked door of Magdalen and I was reading Conrad
when the police were summoned the first time and for the life
of me could see no reason for moving from that door when
the police were summoned a second time I was guilty
of leaving the tradesmans entrance to read Conrad outside
the locked door of Magdalen and I went down with them to sit
in the tradesmans entrance and no one ridiculed me and
for two hours nothing came near me and something out of this
world remembered not recalled survival the wind upon
a wall the Oxford Wall and the only road I came by
white was the wind over the stone of Torre Road Station
and open on the locked door the learning I had come for

July 1985

The Return

in St Johns Wood evening comes slowly to the listless trees
listlessness much the same as that at the edge of Whychwood
only the difference matters and the diurnal form from
which the night takes hold they do not disappear vestigial
here their substance smokes on the skyline reality is
memory the forest trees they do not disappear and
dark is the light within and dark is their hypostasis
though darkness firstly comes to the topmost forest leaves light
comes lastly to the darkest the difference is within and
the difference between futility and despair is the
tree in apparition and the way the night takes hold and
futility is eternal and is not of this world

1985

from **The Pain Clinic Part 1**

I leave behind a poetry from life,
Words and their waiting, words for day and night,
And I have been a mother and a wife
And darkness flaunting seen from depths of light
When dawn's reflection turns the earth below,
The lasting rise of night trees plunged to snow.
Beethoven mapped time a territory fit
For sojourn of the diffident spirit
And Schubert a lyric for love's folly,
Yet love is enough to outlast return
Enough also for love's celibacy
Love is the spirit and its end alone.
I hardly noticed but a love divine
That when Bach spoke at last was lodged with mine.

January 1990

23 Fitzroy Road

I stand before a house and the blue plaque
Of Yeats that drew you without warning or
Omen to that last February dark,
The incongruity of its closed door

And the street leading off into Primrose
Hill spanned almost by a tree's winter girth.
All around the streets circle and enclose
As I struggle with myself, my life's worth
No more than far trees branching from distance
Resolved in a cold without wind or rain,
An emptiness distinct as neon once
Certain, an existence only to drain
Away, while the air heavy with snow's pall
Darkens over the earth and will not fall.

Here, where the high adjacent aviary
Strands its storm over London, caged birds fly
Against the netted turrets endlessly
Encircling an illusion of the sky.
At times I have known this park nearly out
Of my mind with fear, an impossible
Pleading with horizon from fear's redoubt
Always to remain imperceptible.
I wander like Tsvetayeva bereft
Of children and hear in her last tumult
The sound of letting go, like a log left
Behind, time held back in a catapult,
My country has failed to take care of me,
And night the colour of the aviary.

And suddenly the Sibyl of Cumae
Caged among a throng in the market place
To answer to the young 'I want to die',
Where the spirit is the syntax and case
Ending of a poem, death is a shadow
Awaiting its hour, what was a question
Has now become a reality no
Answer could reveal. And from confusion
When even the spirit fails to exist,
Poetry is time's equilibrium,
Through filaments of light, memory missed
Or abandoned, there is a life to come.
You alone sustain and your moon's black hour
Lets fall a snow's indelible shower.

February 1996

Untitled

You stand at the terminus of the one
Three nine and the shops of West End Green are
Closing round us over a reflection
From another time, somewhere in a far
Place other than this where we are patients
Pausing on our way from a nearby day
Hospital, and mourning both for time once
Known and the pain of time to come that lay
As an endless June rain, an evening
Settling softly about us. The same age
And yet the same loss, experiencing
Itself through knowledge that cannot assuage
The emptiness of unborn children or
Those who have grown and gone from the heart's core.

June 1998

Royal Free Hampstead

I watch the day distance itself over
Hampstead Heath and from an open window
Of a psychiatric ward I wonder,
With the last steadfast leaves falling below,
Why am I here? Were the nights as a child
With my mother and our endless journey
Through the streets of Leeds, through desperate wild
Rain, just to end in vain in a room here,
While November trees hold the listless leaves
Held within the first fold of memory,
How the end of a single leaf retrieves
The meaning I have lost, how childhood's key
Is broken fast within its lock, leaves late
In their own stillness falter as I wait.

5th November 1998

Primrose Hill

I do not know where the words will come from
But they come from a time when my mother
Was there, somehow I no longer belong

And yet I am a part of time after,
What am I and what of the time before,
I amount to what I can remember,
Irretrievably lost in the heart's core,
Hidden and left behind in another
Century. I stand alone on Primrose
Hill surrounded by upsurging people
I do not know, locked in a life I chose
Yet without having any choice at all,
And I recognize the writhing trees near
Me in their depiction of the New Year.

31st December, 1999

For John Horder

No one noticed a pool of leftover
Rain, I had one second as we passed by
How I longed to remain, just to linger
There and without anyone asking why
And to see clearly a different kind
Of reality, a world turned upside
Down, infinitesimal blue my mind
Could leap into, a new horizon wide
Open, an imaginary kingdom
Unvisited and yet familiar,
Drawing me with its siren song to come,
To fall without fear into a far
Space as I stood at the edge of the world,
Waiting for language, for the words untold.

23rd April 2001

Dismantling Fordwych House

I am forced to begin a long goodbye,
There is nowhere to go with my sorrow,
The days are just another reason why
Everything that is nurturing must go.
It has sustained me and been a bulwark
Against the world more so a place to be,

Somewhere somehow I was able to work
Drawing pathways into my poetry,
All this will be lost but the fire I drew
Never burnt out, a closed unfolded fan,
Yet high enough to reach into the blue
Sky still whispering of how it began.
There is nowhere else to go to from here,
There is nothing I can do with my fear.

I shall be abandoned by everyone,
And no one will know what is happening,
Left to manage reality alone
Without anything to keep me going,
Most of the time I exist in complete
Despair and hardly able to leave my
Home, the world lies before me at my feet,
The past is an echo answering why.
Trapped between these extremes always, I need
To draw, the finished picture is no more
Than a poultice to draw out pain, to bleed
Into colour again from a far core
In the monochrome region of the mind,
This will cease, it will all be left behind.

And the end is already as a blue
Print now unfolding in its paradigm,
There is nothing that anyone can do,
The dismantling is a matter of time,
And everything I have known will be swept
Away like a carbon copy of my
Life, fugitive in the garden I kept
To, it will not remain however I
Try to keep it from fading forever
In my mind, from the world that was the Art
Room, filtering colours tears and laughter
And lost as an echo left in my heart,
With new lamps for old, I cannot confine
Whatever it was I claimed once as mine.

A resurfacing of a yob culture
I thought to have left forever behind,
An assembly line is the new structure

Based on a working model of a kind,
Allowing respite from extremity
For a single hour only, everything
Else must wait on hold and preferably
With no exception outside the building,
Casual barbarity that never
Should have been allowed through, yet existing
Unopposed without regard for danger,
A regime permitting no resisting,
Either to obey or to go away,
Art therapy will not work in this way.

What is on offer as a replacement
Is but a smoking room in a drop-in
With a pool table, it was never meant
To be anything more than a passing
Remedy for people to sit around
Somehow trying to console each other,
Even they will be sold on and the ground
Reaped for profit, and accepted after
Without a sound for nothing can be done,
We are ill and therefore disenfranchised
And with nothing to lose or to be won.
Is there anyone to have recognised
That this is a proposal that will kill
The most meek and the most vulnerable?

More than fifty places will be reduced
To only fifteen, a day hospital
Razed to the ground, uncertainty unloosed
Where once there was hope and a new level
Of care yet wholly unacceptable
Where the most desperately ill may not
Be allowed to get through, suicidal
Despair may well be turned away with what
Could be termed after as not enough proof.
For some of us the refuge of a ward
Is not possible, for traumatic truth
Experienced there, remains as a sword
In the heart, while the mind left to cower
Each time, is too afraid to remember.

I came to Fordwych House when my own life
Had collapsed, left in utmost jeopardy
In the past, I lived each day on the knife-
Edge of existence with my family
Still around me and gone from me, yet always
In disarray. I knew panic and fear
Again as I had done in the deep maze
Of time and I came when no one was near
Me, left to a fate of insanity,
For me this place was the end of the line.
My first day was the anniversary
Of a poet's death, as though it was mine,
The place then stood between me and my own
Suicide, I felt no longer alone.

The kindness of strangers this was something
I was experiencing for the first
Time but I could only see the ending
Of things, even my shadow was accursed
And I was a fugitive from my own
History, still unable to fit in
Anywhere, yet I belonged there alone
As I was and unable to begin.
And for weeks paralysed before empty
Paper I suddenly began to draw
From a dream under fathoms of the sea
Great stones were grounded on an ocean floor,
Gradually releasing moving free
In rhythms surging continuously.

Five years ago, by then discharged as an
Outpatient, I was allowed to return
For one day a week and slowly began
To draw scenes from my childhood and to learn
From a different angle what the pain
Was like then, the drawings became windows
Each with its own view and I saw again
As though for the first time. An echo throws
A sound that from its first source ricochets
Outward from every surface and forces
Even the silence to listen, the days
After are left without answer, night sees

Another way to apprehend a far
Sound as it draws around a single star.

Sometimes only art therapy got me
Through and for two years after I hardly
Left my flat, nothing worked, I was to be
Marooned and holed up for nine weeks every
Time, leaving mainly out of an utmost
Fear that the day could be taken away
If I left it any longer, yet lost
And bewildered I would go on Thursday
For three or more weeks until the same thing
Started all over again. I got through
In this way and then everything crashed in,
Vestiges of the family I knew
Were gone for ever and I was alone
And left unable to be on my own.

For six months I attended every day
A growing and unmanageable fear
Encompassed me and nothing could allay
Or halt the course of mental nuclear
Meltdown, I was unable to live or
To die, there was nowhere to go, even
Silence such as I had not heard before
Had pushed me over right to the end. When
I was admitted to a ward I felt
That the future was over, time after
Had come to a standstill and days were dealt
Out to me that hardly seemed to matter
Any more, yet at Fordwych House for five
More months I fought each day to stay alive.

I tried for twenty months to keep going,
An infrequent outpatient once again,
I was left outside within a ruin
Inexplicable trying to explain
Without words but the meaning would not come.
I existed in an isolated
World yet unable to trust anyone,
The life I had known was devastated
And not a stone was left to stand or rest

Upon another and there was nothing
Left within, an empty space that oppressed
Me in the dark, a place no scaffolding
Could lean on to, a hollow vacuum
Empty as the days I was lost among.

There is nothing to salvage from those days,
I was on autopilot pretending,
Even reality was a black haze
A smoke engulfing buildings, covering
The sky's rim with an infinite burnt pall.
Each night was a shadow of the unlit
Day in dreams full of clamouring people
Yet indistinct at the furthest limit
Of time, where past and future seem to merge
And the mind is trapped in the interval
Between, forced to the precipitous verge
Of silence and echoes inaudible
Reverberating round an arena,
Locked in an unreachable amnesia.

Poetry had lost its meaning for me,
It had become a weight and a pressure
That I could not bear or carry any-
More, for my mind was ill and beyond cure.
What remained from the years was left behind
As something unknown I turned away from
Suddenly, without looking back, my mind
Was magnified by its own vacuum
And drawn towards the fixed point of the end,
I was alone and out on a far reach
Of time, a one way journey that happened
Almost without my knowing, without search
Or rescue I was beyond horizon,
Turning back was not within my reason.

I could not go back the way I had come
And I could not comprehend the reason
For the journey into the future, some
Remaining knowledge that I was alone
With night coming on and the end before
Me, inexorably there beckoning,

Luring me away from the extinct core
Of the day into the light darkening.
How I wanted to be done with it all,
Just to escape from time coiled around me
After like a tightened spring, to free-fall
Into the timelessness of memory,
An unknown, an inextricable black
Shadow from which there was no turning back.

Nothing else mattered and I sat for days
At a time yet unable to amend
An automatic reflex in the haze
Of green and drifting leaf of an early
Spring, the words had failed and I could not go
On, for my mind was burnt out entirely,
A rudimentary black smoke, hollow
With the sense of something distant and near
With the impact of intangible fear.
The unending planning of how to die
Kept me alive for a little longer,
This was the only certainty and I
Could not allow for anything other
Than a last endless countdown to the end.

June 2001

From The Fields of Killingbeck

How shall I address your silence when I
Cannot confront my own left there to trail
Into the distance as though on stand-by
And as though it is all to no avail.
What remains is a mute reality
Falling backwards with nowhere else to go,
An ebb tide's diminishing entity
Yet leaving me no choice but to follow
Or to stay where I am on an empty
Shore, an interval existing before,
Incising the sea's glass infinity
With an open splintered fallen sun, raw
Levelling in the dark, in a mind's hold,
Lost to the world, locked into the untold.

To confront silence I have to go back
To a dream recurring and coming out
Of nowhere, suddenly taking the lack
Of all the years alone and spent without
You and drawing them into a question
Which you being alive cannot answer.
I try to focus on an illusion
That was to propagate your death after
And leave us in the dark just believing
In what we were told, yet I am distraught
By the truth and continue entreating
You to explain a lie that left us caught
In a time warp with you alive, unknown
To us, and living out your life alone.

It was more real than life itself, a dream
Somehow in which I could believe again
In the time that was left, enough to mean
Something at the end of the years in vain,
Trying to remember you in falling
Rain whenever its ripples spread along
The ground, softly issuing spiralling
Into the light and left there to belong
As they narrowed in the dark to a core
Again. And yet you claimed it was a way
Out to protect us then from an unsure
Future, from knowing that you went away
To live at an address we could not find,
To live you had to leave us all behind.

Whenever I saw you in a dream you
Would always appear as I remembered
You and recovered from your illness through
The years since then, while saying how you led
Us to believe you were dead in order
To be able to leave and to survive,
And I cry we could have known each other
And with the knowledge you were still alive
And I try to tell you how I have missed
All the life we should have had in between,
The joy remains even when you insist
Things were for the best, nothing seems to mean

What it is and I am left with my grief
And the wonder of it in disbelief.

And the dreams were repeated in this way
Until they finally came to an end,
I found it was impossible to say
Anything that would last enough to mend
The endless distance of the years between
That kept us apart in the same city,
With the miracle of your life unseen
Existing without us and suddenly
Quietly about to come to an end.
For you were going to die all over
Again, there was no time left to depend
On, no chance to put it right or alter
Reality, I kept on asking why
There was not enough time to say goodbye.

My disbelief was only the wonder
Of it all, the fact of the narrative
Was the only explanation after
That you did not die but went on to live
Instead, and this was more acceptable
Than the reality of what happened
And what we were left with after, until
The lie on which we had come to depend
Was overturned by a dream. Yet even
They would fail to protect us in the end
And in the last one we only met when
You were about to die, this was the end
Of a dream and they never once returned,
Years passed before I faced what I had learned.

It was too late when we met to have known
Each other even in the make believe
Years of a dream, and in this one alone
You were now dying and about to leave
Me to wonder at the waste of it all.
I kept on saying that you were so near
Why could we not have been told, all the while
Thinking you were dead, living with the fear
That we would never see your face again.

You kept your silence and now there was no
Time left and all the words were just in vain,
What was before us was all we could know,
I learned more about your life from your death
For you seemed to live beyond your last breath.

You were never seen again, you were gone
And the dream disappeared into my mind,
What had once occurred was in some way won
Back from time and became somehow aligned
With the future, events that were able
To mirror each other when turned about
Were lodged forever in a cat's cradle
Where meaning itself was turned inside out,
A dream superseding reality
Because its existence could not be faced
Until the end of years of atrophy
When a dream's last origin could be traced.
The silence of your death was in question
The silence in a dream was my reason.

The sequence of the dreams became a part
Of my existence, a vital refuge
Like softly falling rain, a place to start
From, an anchorage in a centrifuge
Blurring that would never cease to revolve
And yet somewhere I could find you again.
Years melted in the way ripples dissolve
Spiralling back into their core in vain,
In surface currents before and after
Circled outward in a far unbroken
Pattern forcing time into an answer
In the dark, to the locked silence since then.
You told no one and could not reason why
You kept a silence long enough to die.

March 2003

Countertransference

Why am I asked to justify my fear
When interminable memory weighs
Heavy on my mind? My refuge is here
Where I am forced to contend and always
With my back against the wall. Everything
I have known has gone, the familiar
Disappeared long before its echoing
After. In vain I search for the lodestar
Of my being but there is nothing near
Enough to show me where to go, no one
But insubstantial shadows as they veer
Away from me, a collaboration
That would end even as it had begun
With an illusion left to lean upon.

Why can I not be made to feel welcome
Or allowed to come in from the outside
Just to rest awhile as a refuge from
A world where there is nowhere left to hide,
I am a nameless fugitive and mute
With a language known from another time,
Standing my ground with nothing to refute
And rudely pushed away from what is mine.
And yet the pain is something I must bear
Until there is a time to put it down,
Memory loosens its hold and I dare
Not cannot let it go for I shall drown.
There is nothing to bring to ferry me
To the future except disparity.

How casually transference is thrown
Away as though it is of no accord,
Something unfinished with everything known
And left outstanding severed by a sword,
An open wound that will not close again.
There is all the terror of betrayal
Uncoiling like a tightened spring, in vain
The memory and momentum of it all,
Something broken and left in disarray
Even as a far-reaching unending

Amnesia now beginning to set in,
Only the vestiges still remaining
Will last but nothing will ever begin,
Just a feeling of nothing left to say.

How impossible it is from the stand-
Point of a patient even to be heard,
Everything gets turned round on the one hand
And on the other not a single word
Of criticism is allowed except
At the cost of a huge emotional
Affray. Countertransference is adept,
Hiding itself behind a colossal
Smokescreen, a casual play of shadows
Slanting the day, as a deliberate
Subterfuge mimicking loyalty grows
In between the hours, random and innate,
A sense of betrayal the only proof,
The mute fact of feeling, the simple truth.

When I turned around you had disappeared
Before I was aware of your absence,
Something suddenly reached the end and veered
Off leaving without a trace, with a forlorn sense
Of meaning that somehow came to nothing.
My mind hurts with the lasting illusion
Of it all, nothing that is existing
Has any permanence even from one
Day to another, and bound together
By a mute ineffaceable darkness
Woven in between before and after,
As memory begins to coalesce.
In silence since exists the certainty
That you were supposed to be there for me.

It was a belief in you that kept things
Going, though frequently I had to face
That nothing was in place, an echo rings
In my ears beneath the passing surface
Of the years, that this had happened many
Times before. Yet somehow I was always
To mislay my fears, managing any

Leftover doubts, and subsumed in the days
After as something stemming from my own
Sensibility, left there sometimes raw
And over exposed, a figure alone
In a negative aligned in the core
Of light erasing everything before
In the white haze left there after a war.

It was as if the words had been written
Before, as though they had always been there
Waiting to be heard or summoned. Often
I saw them in dreams, a shadow after
And seen suddenly in between the haze
Of another world, silent with their own
Time, trapped in their history, in a maze
Of meaning, an interval unheard shown
In the darkness before it had occurred.
What caused them to align with a sudden
Experience, the mute path hurt and lured
Me back, struggling with something forgotten
And yet awake and using poetry
To sound and encompass reality.

And all the years I had known in the art
Room were overturned and dismantled round
Me, there among the ruins how my heart
Ached for this loss and for time left aground.
The locked unfinished pictures lay before
Me trapped forever in their origin,
Left without any means of rescue or
Release, as something I could imagine
No more. How my senses longed for colour
Even as it began to drain away,
Flowing from the present and the future,
The monochrome of a forgotten day,
With nothing leftover to remember
Me by, to show I had ever been there.

Somewhere along the line the pictures fused
With the poems and I could not explain
How this had occurred or why feeling bruised
The more that memory began to wane,

Until my mind had become an open
Wound, a narrow fissure on the surface
Of a timeless vacuum that often
Seemed about to explode under the trace
Of something existing and beforehand,
With nothing in place to ease the pressure
Enough to be able to understand
The far monochrome region at the core
Of being, the sunless light in a dream
In the starless darkness of things that seem.

Even the pictures were seen before they
Were drawn, locked somewhere fast where I could not
Reach them, and existing so far away
That only in the finished picture what
I had seen then, became perceptible
Triggering memory from long ago,
An experience lodged in the shortfall
Of time, there leaning on its own shadow,
A sense of something waiting to happen
As though the end itself was left on hold
And waiting for me to catch up, often
Allowing me to hold something untold
And unrealised, balancing its load,
With destiny left in the stand-by mode.

All the years just came to a standstill,
There in the art room where the atmosphere
Without warning was unmanageable,
When nothing was allowed to interfere
With the headlong momentum of something
Beneath the surface closing the foreground,
The sound of confrontation echoing
Without end, a reality that wound
Itself around me until I was bound
About in its inexorable hold,
There waylaid even as I ran aground
By language alone and what the words told.
And seven years were as though they never
Existed, either before or after.

The confrontation when it came about
Was final and sudden and everything
Was left resounding in its wake without
Recourse to reason, any suffering
Was ignored then and there, for it could all
Be put down to an overreaction,
But what was lost was irretrievable.
An overriding faith in someone known
Was gone, and my mind had been pushed too far
And the years collapsed and came to an end,
Abandoned and now unfamiliar
And then as a future I could depend
On no more, a structure insubstantial,
No more than an interval left to stall.

This was a rerun of two months before,
And now I was trying to repair it
Again but this time there was nothing more
To be done, the wound was a direct hit
And there was no way out, I could not go
On pretending I was wanted any
More. In vain I tried to say there was no
Way I could speak about my pain, many
Times people were allowed to pressurise
Me in the group, it seemed they were going
In for the kill, I could not recognise
The art therapist who kept insisting
On a reply as though I must answer
For my pain beyond before or after.

It was open season, people could say
What they wanted but I was not allowed
To remain silent or in any way
Prevent it happening, there in the crowd
It seemed that the only thing to be done
Was to flee in tears distraught from the art
Room. So many were the times lost among
The years I had left there coming apart,
Only to return again with self blame
Knowing well that nothing could be explained,
This time nothing would ever be the same,
The door was to close as the future waned

In the distance, as I was turned away
For remaining there with nothing to say.

It took seven years to get rid of me,
So strong was my capacity to cling
On for the sake of the pictures and only
By turning a blind eye could anything
Be accomplished there. Yet art therapy
Was the one way out of an endless maze,
Colour that veered off into poetry
Was left to drain away through those last days
Until all that was left was a black space,
A burnt-out uncontrollable feeling
That the void I would leave on the surface
Of the paper was the heart of being,
The extinct core seen in a dream as though
In the light I became my own shadow.

Colour drained away in much the same way
Almost two years before when as a last
Resort to try to save the art room, day
By day I went without food in a fast
That was to last for three months, at the end
Of which Fordwych House was allowed to stay
As it was. But the joy could not amend
The weeks of pain that would not go away,
That flowed into the protest that followed
In the nine months after, hunger reduced
Colour to a hollow spectrum, a mode
Of darkness encompassed by a sealed fused
Light leaving me with no way out and like
The monochrome hours of a hunger strike.

April 2003

Nameless in Camden

They come to me like wraiths out of the mist,
Lost, insignificant, the dispossessed
Searching for their shadow mislaid or missed,
Effaced from the day. They linger oppressed
Without end with the knowledge of someone
Since forgotten that will not go away,
They pass with only their own reflection
For consolation outstaring the day,
The outlandish night left there, endlessly
Merging as an early oblivion
And into everything they cannot see.
And sometimes in dreams, in low light unshone,
From echoes remembered something is heard
Yet recurring mnemonic and conferred.

31st October-6th November 2003

They trace the heel of the day forever
In front, with something of a life straight from
The heart as they react between after
And before, held in its arc as they come
And go with a truth that has come apart
And a name's echo they cannot go back
To, a future that refuses to start,
That stalling lies abandoned in its track.
The last light of a day is all there is
Left, the sudden footsteps falling away,
Throbbing endlessly through the arteries
Of a life on hold with nowhere to lay
Its head, hollowing out a centrifuge,
An open dark without any refuge.

7th-12th November 2003

MICHAEL WILLIAMS

Old Woman

Old woman
you passed my side
and within the
time of that
moment
I felt a great
pulse of my heart

You walk the cold
pathways without
guide or staff
knowing cataract
scars
keeps your purse
in deep wrath

So dodging are
your steps
yet regal your
walk
heroine of hurts
of this life
before death

I marvel your
stance
so shunning to
fear
indifferent to
where
or what without
pillow
Held high is your
head
so obedient to you
dressed between
those changes
of sun and moon

Seals of age
politics of rags
tapestry of wet
mornings
weaved in solitude

Beatitude of stitches
stitches of before
locked within secret
in the folds of torn
scarves

I saw you lady
I breathed your style
giving me purpose
to think my life
again

Old woman
you passed my side
and within the time
of that moment
I felt I was born

Old woman
you passed my side
turning into a corner
and then you were gone

Old woman
you are with me still.

LEE WILSON

The Eternal Camera

And here's one of her knelt before that mosaic -
red-eye over the shoulder. She'd run her finger
around a single tessera's pixel of time
in a fashion known to her own skin,
in its gratitude for the eye - bloated
with what there's conspiracy to call lust -
that grants her absence from eternity.
Because, to be caught in a stance,
of love, or allegiance,
her brow and palm-lines sketching ripples
fleeing the disturbed heart -
all things considered, she'd rather not.

But doesn't the eye
the desperate church sold,
worked now into a millionaire's floor, still see
the pews, the damp doubtful blinking
behind the genuflexion, the rock
it was, the axe the slave swung?

There is in this stolen snapshot
a double exposure: clearly visible
the Big Bang itself, each quark
looking back mortified
into the aperture, at the hope
they hadn't the patience to sustain.

JUNE WORSELL

Dandelions

They glowed along the wayside edge,
Like studs amid the dusty grass.
Long the mile they walked with me,
With a shine like leaded glass.
then as they reached the village road.
thwarted by grimy tarmac.
There they bid a brief farewell.
One leap and they were back.
They danced tall upon the village green,
But short upon the lawn.
Smiled sweetly in my flower bed
where fluffy seeds were borne.

The Crimson Rose

Before me in a jar, a crimson rose.
Clothed by Gods own draper.
Fool as I am, but still I try,
To capture her image on paper.

I paint the first whorl of crimson petals,
But my velvet lay's without a nap.
I lean back at my creations life giving stem,
Yet it contains no spring or vital sap.

Her saw like edges on dark green leaves,
placed so uniformly and precise,
Delicate veins of pale; fine threads,
If only mine looked half as nice.

Where she breathes hypnotic perfume;
Which floats invisibly on the air
Although my rose takes on her shape and form
There's not a hint of scent, so I can't compare.

On a petal I craft a drop of dew,
Yet fail to trap the rainbow in,
My feeble effigy to a thorn,
Has not the power to pierce the skin

I did not see her defences drawn,
As I reached out for the bud.
She left her statement on my painting,
A final flourish, in my crimson blood.

JOHN YOUNGER

Case History

The opthalmologist's report
of retinal damage was terse
and technical. It rests in his files,
silent on how it felt
when blood began to fill my eyes.

Picnicking at Far Moorside with friends,
summer sun encouraged ease, until
a blot defaced the landscape's page
Soon others splashed across the afternoon
patterning the scene with random threats.

Faster, in the weeks that followed,
leaking blood burst through again
and sight began to drown, entangled
with strings of long black weed,
in an underwater world.

Where depths below depths obscure,
pressure on the optic nerves
make bright shapes swim
from nowhere through the brain,
to float, divide, then coalesce and fade.

Now, in the disorder's final stage,
sunk from daylight's certainty
to the bottom of a lake of darkness,

the struggle to surface and survive
means living treading water.

American Dreams

In Henry James' short story
'The Jolly Corner', 1908,
a man, shielding a candle flame's shiver,
nightly searches the empty rooms
of his Fifth Avenue house -

driven to confront the shape
he knows is haunting them.
They meet darkly, but lit enough
for him to recognise
a damaged, dangerous future self
he may escape, within his author's
imagination of disaster.
Real life sixty-seven years later
and artist Andy Warhol daily
patrols his East Side mansion,
unlocking rooms crammed with purchases
he peers at, before locking up again.
At night, unlocking doors once more
he switches on the lights, repeating
the morning ritual, but doesn't seek
a future self- already present.
Fictional and realnon, both figures
share a dream, whatever
ghosts pursued by or pursuing.

Acknowledgements

Our thanks to Julia Blackburn for Thomas Blackburn, to Gallery Press for James Simmons, to Hamish MacGibbon for Stevie Smith, to Peter Porter for Martin Bell and to the writers themselves for all others. We are very sorry but in a number of cases we have tried to trace copyrights without success. We will put this right in future editions if we are contacted.